YOUNG JEFFERSON

Thomas Fleming

1

D own a narrow, rutted dirt road, past fields where brown tobacco leaves mellowed in the sun, rode a rangy, rusty-haired man of twenty-seven on a muscular bay horse. The man was in an exuberant mood. His blue-gray eyes devoured the vivid colors of the changing woods in the rich fall sunshine. Other travelers on the road got a cheerful good morning. Occasionally, he would hum a song.

None of this was unusual. Thomas Jefferson was fond of saying: "There is not a sprig of grass that grows uninteresting to me." He could give without hesitation the ponderous botanical names for almost every tree and bush he passed. As a true-born Virginian, he was proud, too, of his courtesy.

It did not matter if a fellow traveler was black and a slave. Each person Jefferson met received the same gracious, soft-voiced greeting. As for humming songs, this long-limbed "straight-up" six-footer was always singing as he strode about his plantation.

Even more than most Virginians of his day, Thomas Jefferson loved music. A few feet behind the young lawyer rode his slave, Jupiter, the guardian of Jefferson's most precious possession - his violin. It may have been Jupiter who nine months before rode frantically into Charlottesville to bring Jefferson the worst possible news. His family home, Shadwell, had been destroyed by a wind-whipped fire. In anguish, Jefferson asked if anything - above all his 1,000-book library - had been rescued. "No, marster, all lost," was the reply, "but we save your fiddle."

Most of the melodies Tom Jefferson was humming on this journey in the fall of 1770 were love songs. The words were absurd, in the plaintive romantic tradition of the day.

Enraptured I gaze when my Delia is by

And drink the sweet poison of love from her eye;

I feel the soft passion pervade every part

And pleasures unusual play 'round my fond heart.

A few months before, this young man of the world

would have laughed cynically at such bathos. But now he was on his way to make his first visit to a house called The Forest. A tall, rather ungainly wooden structure, it sat on a knoll overlooking the broad James River, the main highway of Virginia that flowed serenely from Richmond to the sea. The great planters of the Old Dominion - the Carters, the Shirleys, the Randolphs - had far more magnificent houses, near-palaces of resplendent red brick. Only a mile and a half from The Forest was one of the finest, Shirley, where the agreeable and well-known Jefferson would have been equally welcome. But The Forest was his destination on this fine October day. There was someone waiting there who seemed to listen with a special attention to the young attorney's strenuous opinions on topics as various as slavery, architecture, the political rights of colonial Americans, and the importance of scientific farming.

Her name was Martha Wayles Skelton and her hair was a rich auburn, her large eyes hazel. A fragile, diminutive beauty of twenty-two, she was the widow of Bathhurst Skelton, one of a lively group of young men with whom Tom Jefferson had shared his student days at the College of William and Mary in Williamsburg. He had probably met Martha Wayles then, along with a host of other girls whose names still twinkle in his youthful letters - Rebecca Burwell, Suzanna Potter, Alice Corbin, Nancy Randolph. Jefferson had spent the years between twenty and twenty-three adoring Rebecca, an orphan descended from some of the best families of Virginia. The heiress to a considerable fortune, Rebecca lived with the wealthy William Nelsons of Yorktown.

"Enthusiasm" was the word her contemporaries used to sum up Rebecca in later years. To the eighteenth century, this meant a vivid, strongly emotional personality. For months, Jefferson had carried with him in his watch a silhouette of her that she had cut out with her own hands - surely a sign that she did not treat his courtship with complete disdain. But this memento met a fate that might have made a more superstitious man suspect worse disasters to come. Visiting over the Christmas holidays with another set of friends, Jefferson put the watch containing "the dear picture," as he called it, on a table beside his bed. During the night, it rained. Jefferson woke to find his watch "all afloat in water" let in by a leak in the roof. When he attempted to rescue Rebecca's image from the deluge, his "cursed fingers" gave it a rip that fatally mangled it.

For over two years, the romance percolated, but Jefferson could not seem to bring himself to ask the ultimate question. He rhapsodized in letters about "Belinda" - the romantic name he gave Rebecca in the vain hope of disguising her identity among his friends - but he knew that marriage in eighteenth-century Virginia meant the end of youth, a sad farewell to the bachelor's freedom. For Jefferson, it would also mean the extinction of his dream of traveling to that distant, fascinating old world of England, France, and Italy, about which he had read so much.

Once, alone with Rebecca in a garden, he had hinted strongly that if she would promise to wait a year or two, he would begin his grand tour instantly. But the young lady's frown seemed to cast a shadow on this idea. The would-be lawyer returned to his struggles with "Old Coke," as he called Sir Edward Coke, the great British jurist whose commentaries on the laws of England were famed for their crabbed style and "uncouth but cunning learning." Retreating to Shadwell, Jefferson lamented that he was certain to spend his time thinking of Rebecca "too often, I fear, for my peace of mind, and too often, I am sure, to get through Old Cooke [Coke] this winter: for God knows I have not seen him since I packed him up in my trunk in Williamsburg."

A month later, he was writing to his same friend, John Page, asking plaintively, "How does RB do? What do you think of my affair, or what would you advise me to do? Had I better stay here and do nothing or go down and do less?" He decided on the first choice and spent his days and nights struggling with Coke and planning a voyage in an imaginary ship called *The Rebecca* in which he would visit "England, Holland, France, Spain, Italy (where I would buy me a good fiddle), and Egypt."

Meanwhile, another college mate, Jacquelin Ambler, began visiting Jefferson's unattainable damsel. All through the following spring and summer, Jefferson stayed home and philosophized: "If she consents, I shall be happy; if she does not, I must endeavor to be so as much as possible . . . Perfect happiness, I believe, was never intended by the Deity to be the lot of any one of his creatures in this world."

His friend Page, acting both as adviser and ambassador, warned Jefferson that Ambler was making ominous progress. So at last the philosophic lover bestirred himself and came down to Williamsburg for the social season. He was soon giving Ambler strong competition.

Then came a climactic night at Raleigh Tavern, the favorite gathering place of the young bloods and their belles. The tables were cleared, and the ladies and gentlemen arrived for a ball. The ladies were dressed "in that gay and splendid" style that made Virginia famous, their hair "craped" high with rolls on each side, topped by caps of gauze and lace. The men looked nearly as splendid in their clockwork silk stockings, lace ruffles, gold-and silver-laced cocked hats, and breeches and waistcoats of blue, green, scarlet, or peach. The idea was to see and be seen, to charm and be charmed.

Jefferson had spent the hours before the dance

composing a whole series of romantic compliments, witty remarks, and bright observations. "I was prepared to say a great deal," he told his friend Page. "I had dressed up in my own mind such thoughts as occurred to me in as moving language as I knew how and expected to have performed in a tolerably creditable manner."

But when Jefferson came face to face with Rebecca in all her finery, he told Page later: "Good God! ... a few broken sentences uttered in great disorder and interrupted with pauses of uncommon length were the too visible marks of my strange confusion!"

"Last night," the vanquished suitor lamented, "I never could have thought the succeeding sun would have seen me so wretched as I now am!"

Behind the mask of the blithe bachelor and engaging young lawyer, there was concealed a deeply sensitive, essentially shy scholar.

The following May, Rebecca married Jacquelin Ambler, and Jefferson retired once more to philosophizing and making matches for his friends. He even proposed to Suckey Potter on behalf of his fellow lawyer William Fleming. A few lines later he was telling Will, "Many and great are the comforts of a single state, and neither of the reasons you urge can have any influence with an inhabitant and a young inhabitant too of Wmsburg."

A few weeks later he was cheerfully reporting to Page

the fate of their friend Warner Lewis: "Poor fellow, never did I see one more sincerely captivated in my life. He walked to Indian Camp with her yesterday, by which means he had an opportunity of giving her two or three love squeezes by the hand, and like a true Arcadian swain, has been so enraptured ever since that he is company for no one."

But such examples of romantic bliss did not impress Jefferson. After his narrow escape, he settled down to practicing law and enjoying life. He dated his Williamsburg letters "Devilsburgh" and needled friends such as Fleming for falling in love. Jefferson even drifted in a direction more than one bachelor has taken and made wry comments on the matchmaking all around him. When William Bland won Betsey Yates, Jefferson wryly remarked: "Whether it was for money, beauty, or principle, it will be so nice a dispute that no one will venture to pronounce."

Soon he was copying from his favorite books quotations that trace an equally familiar evolution of the bachelor's psychology.

. . . Wed her?

No! Were she all desire could wish, as fair

As would the vainest of her sex be thought

With wealth beyond what woman's pride could waste

She should not cheat me of my freedom . . .

He placed more and more value on the company of his men friends, conveniently ignoring the fact that most of them had married. One day he was writing John Page about how much he enjoyed "the philosophical evenings" at Page's plantation, Rosewell. The next day, he was copying: "I'd leave the world for him that hates a woman, woman the fountain of all human frailty."

The remarks about frailty may have special significance. Around this time, the roving bachelor became involved in a flirtation that he was to regret bitterly in future years. One of his close friends in his native Albemarle County was Jack Walker. He had married a buxom miss named Betsey Moore and was living only a few miles from the Jeffersons' home. Walker had been offered the job of clerk to a Virginia commission negotiating a treaty with the Indians at Fort Stanwix, and he departed for this post beyond the Blue Ridge Mountains, leaving Betsey behind.

Jefferson knew Betsey and was a frequent visitor in the Walkers' home, as he was in the houses of all his married friends. But for Betsey and him, the visits suddenly became more than casual meetings. It was the theme of which popular fiction has long been made: the lonely bride, the lonelier bachelor, and the unsuspecting absent husband. Before long, a mixture of passion and calculation had Jefferson using his college education to persuade Betsey that there was nothing whatsoever wrong with enjoying the delights of illicit love. To back him up, he undoubtedly quoted poets and novelists by the yard. But Betsey, after hesitating long enough to send the bachelor into a frenzy of woman-hating, finally said no, and Jefferson retreated with nothing to show for his efforts but a badly wounded ego.

Fortunately, there came into his lovelorn life a far more healthy influence. He had another boyhood friend from Albemarle - one much closer than Jack Walker. His name was Dabney Carr. Like Jefferson, he, too, was pursuing the law as a career and showed great promise. In 1765, Carr married Jefferson's younger sister Martha. Their happiness made a deep impression on Jefferson and all but reversed his plunge into cynicism. To his favorite correspondent, John Page, Jefferson wrote, almost wonderingly, about how Carr "speaks, thinks and dreams of nothing but his young son. This friend of ours, Page, in a very small house, with a table, half a dozen chairs, and one or two servants, is the happiest man in the universe."

Seeing Page himself happily married with two fine children and a wife who shared his fondness for books and good talk also impressed Jefferson. After a 1770 visit to Rosewell, the Page estate, he wrote: "I was always fond of philosophy even in its dryer forms, but from a ruby lip it comes with charms irresistible. Such a feast of sentiment must exhilarate life . . . at least as much as the feast of the sensualist shortens it."

Seven months after he wrote these words, Jefferson was riding blissfully toward The Forest singing love songs. In Martha Wayles Skelton, he had found a woman who totally routed the potential cynic in his nature. "Sweetness of temper" was the quality Jefferson put first in a list of wifely virtues he compiled for one of his numerous notebooks. This, Martha Wayles possessed to an extraordinary degree. Among her other qualities, two were especially attractive to a sophisticated young Virginian of 1770 - "spriteliness and sensibility." In Virginia, as in Europe, there was a growing fondness for the romantic in contrast to the coldly classical formalism that had dominated literature and the arts for most of the eighteenth century. The newest style was to be a person of sensibility and to react with strong emotions to the beauties and pleasures of life, to its joy and sadness. One Virginia belle proudly reported to a friend her reaction to the latest work of the popular novelist, Lady Julia Mandeville: "I think I never cried more in my life reading a novel."

What delight it must have been for Jefferson when he discovered that he and Martha shared a common enthusiasm for *Tristram Shandy* by Laurence Sterne. This comic masterpiece was the black humor of its day, considered just a little naughty by the strait-laced, but fervently admired by the younger generation for the way it spoofed musty academic learning, windy doctors of medicine, boring old soldiers, and a dozen other favorite satiric targets of the young, while pausing to bathe in pure sentiment such inevitabilities as true love and premature death.

The philosophy of the book is clear in Sterne's dedication: "I live in a constant endeavor to fence against the infirmities of ill health and other evils of life by mirth; being firmly persuaded that every time a man smiles - but much more so when he laughs, that it adds something to this Fragment of Life."

Martha Skelton's fondness for *Tristram Shandy* was not her only recommendation. She also shared Jefferson's passion for music and played beautifully on the spinet and harpsichord. Add to these accomplishments a natural grace, a brilliant complexion, large, expressive hazel eyes, and thick hair with a tinge of auburn, and it is obvious why Thomas Jefferson was wearing out his horseflesh on the road to The Forest.

He soon discovered there were other suitors. Martha was not only beautiful; she was rich. Her father was, in Jefferson's words, "a lawyer of much practice" who had amassed a handsome fortune, and she had inherited still more wealth from her two years of marriage with Bathhurst Skelton. Between her late husband, dead now two years, and her father, she would eventually own over 10,000 acres of prime Virginia land. Such a prize whetted the ardor of more than one young scion. But Jefferson soon forged ahead of the other eager visitors. At twenty-seven, he was already a member of the House of Burgesses, Virginia's legislature, and a well-established lawyer making $3,000 a year from his practice at the bar and $2,000 from his 5,000 acres of good farmland. This was a substantial income in the days when a laborer could be hired for as little as $10 a month.

There is a tradition that her industrious father had trained Martha "to business" and this gave Jefferson another advantage. Martha was supposedly looking for a husband who could manage her substantial estate. A far wealthier Virginia widow, Martha Custis, had thus combined heart and head when she married Colonel George Washington in 1759. But there is no evidence of such a sensible, if not inspiring explanation for Jefferson's success. On the contrary, there is far more evidence that between Martha Wayles Skelton and Thomas Jefferson the dominant emotion was deep, compelling love.

But as a woman of sensibility and a true Virginia belle, Martha was not about to capitulate immediately to Jefferson. A girl in 1770 Virginia was expected to keep a suitor dangling for six or eight months at least. Martha did better than that, although it was not entirely her fault.

Twice before the year 1770 ended, Jefferson returned to The Forest, finally spending the Christmas holidays there. By the time he rode away, after sharing this jolliest of seasons on a Virginia plantation, he no longer had the slightest doubt that he and Martha were deeply in love. But he was confronted by an unexpected reluctance on the part of John Wayles to accept him as a son-in-law.

Just why is something of a mystery. Perhaps Wayles had higher social ambitions for his daughter. As a lawyer who was, in Jefferson's own words, "welcomed in every society," he may have envisioned a family alliance between his line and one of the aristocratic Virginia families whose great estates dotted the banks of the lower James.

Jefferson's maternal lineage was good enough. His mother had been a Randolph, definitely one of the first families of the colony. But by 1770, the Randolphs had multiplied so prodigiously that a descent on the maternal side did not mean much. William Randolph of Turkey Island, who died in 1711, had been a man of vast wealth and energy. He had seven sons, and they, in turn, married and begat and acquired more wealth with all of their father's zest. By the end of the eighteenth century, so many people were involved in the Randolph line that despairing genealogists called William and his wife "the Adam and Eve of Virginia."

The Jeffersons, on the other hand, were much more obscure. They were descended from Thomas Jefferson I, who came to Virginia about 1679 and died in 1697. They never acquired vast swaths of prime Virginia land as the Randolph males did. The Jeffersons moved west in search of cheaper land, in the manner of millions of Americans in generations to come, until they reached Albemarle County where they achieved a sturdy prosperity. However, in 1770, Albemarle was still considered, if not the frontier, definitely back country, one of the less socially attractive parts of the state. In later years, Jefferson was to refer acidly to the "cyphers of the aristocracy" who controlled Virginia in his youth - a hint that he may have more than once endured some painful comparisons with these elegant families. At any rate, on February 20, 1771, he was complaining to a friend about how the "unfeeling temper of a parent" could obstruct a marriage.

Nevertheless, Jefferson never let John Wayles's attitude discourage him. Seldom did two weeks go by without seeing Jefferson and Jupiter ride up the hill to hand their horses over to the stable boys at The Forest. It was during one of these visits, family tradition tells us, that two other suitors arrived not long after Jefferson. They were preening themselves on the broad veranda, getting ready to make their entrance, when from inside the house there came the sound of a violin and a spinet playing a plaintive love song. For a long moment, the two suitors stood there eying each other uneasily. Without a word, they went down the steps, recalled their horses from the stables and rode away. Something about the duet made it clear that they were wasting their time.

Jefferson made no secret of his love. In August 1771, he was telling another frequent visitor to The Forest, Robert Skipwith, who was courting Martha's younger sister Tabitha, to "offer prayers for me at that shrine to which though absent I pray continual devotions. In every scheme of happiness, she is placed in the foreground of the picture, as the principal figure. Take that away, and it is no picture for me."

He was also singing Martha's praises in Williamsburg, as is evident from a letter he received in the spring of 1771 from an older woman friend, Mrs. Drummond. She was obviously still breathless from a word picture of Martha the capitulated bachelor had left with her. "Let me recollect your discription," she wrote, "which bars all the romantic poetical ones I ever read . . . Thou wonderful young man, indeed I shall think spirits of an higher order inhabits yr aerey mountains - or rather mountain, which I may contemplate but never can aspire too . . . Persevere, thou good young man, persevere - she has good sence and good nature, and I hope will not refuse (the blessing shal' I say) why not as I think it, - of yr hand, if her heart's not ingagd allready."

The "aerey mountain" Mrs. Drummond mentioned with such admiration was a conical 857-foot peak little more than a mile outside Charlottesville, soaring in lonely splendor above the broad Piedmont Valley. When he was still in his teens, Jefferson and Dabney Carr used to ramble the slopes of this oddly isolated little mountain that was part of the Jefferson property. They would sit by the hour beneath the shade of a great oak, exchanging visionary plans of the future. Once, in a sentimental moment, they promised each other that if one died young, the survivor would see to it that he was buried here, beneath the brooding shadows of the great tree's sun-dappled branches. But Jefferson found the crest of the mountain more exhilarating and here, he impulsively told Carr one day, he planned to build a house. In eighteenth-century Virginia, with its all but nonexistent roads and dependence on river transportation, this was an idea almost as fanciful as flying.

The idea might have remained a boyish dream if fire had not destroyed Shadwell. Earlier biographers had pictured this first home as a rude cabin in the wilderness. Recent archeological research on the site now makes it clear that Shadwell was a spacious country house, a rival, if not an equal, to The Forest and similar family estates. Shadwell's ruins revived Jefferson's dream of a more magnificent mansion on the nearby mountain. Soon he had workmen clearing and leveling the summit of the conical height.

Building was a slow business in the eighteenth century. After more than a year of work, all Jefferson was able to finish was a one-room brick cottage. But by now, he was so much in love with his mountain that he moved into this tiny abode. In February 1771, he was cheerfully writing to a friend that his one room, "like the cobbler's, serves me for parlour, for kitchen and hall, I may add for bed chamber and study too . . . I have hope, however, of getting more elbow room this summer."

This casual phrase was light-years away from the magnificent house Jefferson had already sketched and planned down to the precise proportions of every room. He was determined to create a house that blended the spirit of America and the architectural genius of Europe. Part of his motive was patriotic pride. He winced at most of the houses he saw in Virginia. The typical country house was usually constructed by the plantation owner himself, sometimes with the aid of a professional builder. The only architectural plans consulted, if any, were dull copies of English models. Except for a few great mansions such as Carter's Grove, near Williamsburg, most houses were unimaginative boxlike wooden squares or rectangles, with small ugly windows and low ceilings, their interiors haphazardly divided into smaller squares and rectangles. "It was impossible to devise things more ugly, [and] uncomfortable," Jefferson said. It cost nothing to add "symmetry and taste." But alas, there was "scarcely a model" in Virginia "sufficiently chaste to give an idea of them."

Already Jefferson had grasped the insight that was to make him the father of American architecture. In his college days, he had discovered the great Renaissance architect, Andrea Palladio, who had studied in detail the Roman ruins of Italy to learn the principles of his art. Jefferson instinctively responded to this classic tradition with its emphasis on clean, chaste lines and carefully calculated symmetry. Not only did the style have "the approbation of thousands of years," but it was a perfect model for men struggling to bring order out of a chaotic wilderness. At the same time, Jefferson's American instincts set his house on a hill, where the eye could roam over miles of open country to the misty Blue Ridge Mountains where the frontier began. The reconciliation of freedom and order - the theme that was to absorb Thomas Jefferson's life - was symbolized here in its beginning years at Monticello.

American, too, was Jefferson's taste when it came to gardening. He liked contrast, mixture, in art and envisioned his classic house surrounded by free-form gardens in the "Gothic" or natural style. His romantic state of mind obviously had something to do with this preference. In the summer of 1770, when he was urging his friend Skipwith to offer prayers for him at The Forest, he was sketching plans for a garden that included "a temple beside a spring" and a handy harp to add plaintive music.

In his woman-hating bachelor days, Jefferson had named his mountain "The Hermitage." Now, he began calling it "Monticello" - which means "little mountain" in Italian and is pronounced "Montichello." No doubt it came from his books on Palladio. But the chief appeal of the name was its sweetly romantic ring.

All this romantic staging meant little unless Jefferson remembered Mrs. Drummond's advice to persevere. So he continued to pay frequent visits to The Forest. From England, he ordered an expensive "forte-piano" - the very latest in musical improvements. He made a point of insisting "the workmanship of the whole [be] very handsome and worthy of the acceptance of a lady for whom I intend it." He also asked half humorously if his British agent would search the herald's office for the arms of the Jefferson family. "It is possible there may be none," he wrote. "If so, I would with your assistance become a purchaser, having Sterne's word for it that a coat of arms may be purchased as cheap as any other coat."

Jefferson was obviously straining to persuade someone - if not Martha, her father - that there was some worthwhile lineage on the Jefferson side of the argument too.

That he was making progress is evident from a letter written to him by Robert Skipwith in September of 1771. After thanking Jefferson for speaking affectionately of his "dearest Tibby," Skipwith expressed a wistful desire to "be neighbors to a couple so well calculated and disposed to communicate knowledge - and pleasure. My sister Skelton, Jefferson I wish it were, has all the qualities which promise to assure you the greatest happiness mortals are capable of enjoying. May business and play musick and the merriments of your family companions lighten your hearts, soften your pillows and procure you health, long life and every human felicity!" Obviously, only the "unfeeling parent" needed to be worn down, to win the prize.

On November 11, 1771, if we interpret rightly the little pocket account book Jefferson kept, John Wayles finally agreed to surrender his daughter. The wedding date was set for January 1, little more than six weeks away and proof of the couple's impatience. As the elated suitor departed for Monticello, he shared his joy with the Wayles's servants. Jefferson had always tipped them; it was the custom on Virginia plantations. But his amounts had been moderate, as befitted a sensible man who came and went regularly. Now he threw pounds and shillings right and left with an abandon that sent toasts to Jefferson echoing around The Forest's black quarter for the rest of the week.

What a ride back to Monticello Jupiter must have had, thundering over those atrocious roads in Jefferson's reckless wake. From boyhood, Jefferson had been a fearless rider, always choosing the best blood horses, which he broke himself. Instead of letting Jupiter lead his horse across the Rivanna River while he took a boat, Jefferson invariably plunged into this treacherous little stream that he always had to cross on journeys to and from Monticello. Even when the river was swollen by spring rains and the horse had to swim for his life, Jefferson scorned the ferry.

Time was short, and there was much to be done. Monticello had to be made as habitable as possible for the bride. In spite of the wintry weather, orders were issued to push hard on the construction of the main house, which had several rooms more or less completed. There were presents to be bought, guest lists to be drawn up, and plans to be made for transporting Jefferson's mother, his four sisters, and his brother to the wedding.

On December 23, the all-but-ex-bachelor was back at The Forest to sign a very English-sounding wedding bond. His cosigner Francis Eppes was Martha's brother-in-law.

> Know all men by these presents that we
> Thomas Jefferson and Francis Eppes are held
> and firmly bound to our Sovereign Lord the
> King, his heirs and successors in the sum of

fifty pounds current money of Virginia . . .
The condition of the above obligation is such
that if there be no lawful cause to obstruct a
marriage intended to be had and solemnized
between the above bound Thomas Jefferson
and Martha Skelton of the County of Charles
City, widow, for which a license is desired,
then this obligation is to be null and void;
otherwise to remain in full force.

Jefferson paid the forty shillings for the marriage
license and in the next eight days no "lawful cause"
turned up to prevent the consummation of his
dreams. No less than two ministers presided at
the ceremony, each of whom Jefferson paid five
pounds. There were fiddlers, also well paid by
the bridegroom, and it is certain that everyone
devoured a sumptuous slice of a rich black wedding
cake made with pounds of fruit, wine, brandy, and
dozens of eggs. The guests had traveled for days to
enjoy the festivities, and enjoy them they did - for
the next two and a half weeks. Not until January 18
did the newlyweds set out for Monticello, and even
then they were in no hurry to get there.

On the way, Jefferson made a sentimental stop
at Tuckahoe, the Randolph estate on the James a
few miles above Richmond. The old white frame
house with brick ends forming a letter H was
rich in memories for him. For seven years, Tom
Jefferson had lived there as a schoolboy, while his

father, Peter Jefferson, had administered the estate and acted as guardian for the orphaned family of his friend and in-law William Randolph. Jefferson often said that his earliest memory was the day he was carried on a pillow by a mounted slave from Shadwell to Tuckahoe. Because William Randolph had stipulated in his will that his son, Thomas Mann Randolph, was to be taught by tutors, young Tom Jefferson also received his first schooling in a little house that still stands in the yard of Tuckahoe.

Jefferson made Martha laugh heartily with tales of those primitive school days. He loved to tell how once, when he was desperate with hunger, he repeated the Lord's Prayer in the hope of speeding the arrival of the dinner hour.

Tuckahoe also revived fond memories of Peter Jefferson, that giant of a man who had slept beneath Virginia's soil for almost fifteen years now. This huge pioneer, who had ventured into Albemarle when there were less that fifty white men living in the vicinity, was a kind of legend to Jefferson. He often told of the time his father was directing three able-bodied slaves to pull down a ruined shed with a rope. The slaves hauled and sweated, and nothing happened. Peter Jefferson seized the rope, slung it over one massive shoulder, and gave a mighty heave. In an instant, the shed was kindling on the ground. They still talked in Albemarle of his most fantastic feat, simultaneously "heading up" (raising from their sides to an upright position) two hogsheads of tobacco weighing nearly 1,000 pounds apiece.

As a surveyor, Peter Jefferson had done as much as any man in Virginia to lay out the boundaries of the colony and construct a workable map. He had fought his way through the winter wilderness, leaving behind him a trail of assistants collapsed from starvation and fatigue, often living on the raw flesh of game and even on his own pack-train mules, sleeping in hollow trees while wolves and wildcats howled around him.

This same man went back to his plantation and read Addison, Swift, Pope and, above all, Shakespeare. Though he had died when Thomas was only fourteen, Peter Jefferson had already passed on to his son a vivid heritage. One of his favorite maxims was, "Never ask another to do for you what you can do for yourself." He made sure his son knew how to sit a horse, ford a swollen river, fire a gun, and fight his way up and down wooded hills in pursuit of deer and wild turkey. At the same time, he insisted with ferocity on Tom's obtaining the best possible education. In the course of a rugged life, he himself had had to snatch his learning whenever and wherever he could.

Tom Jefferson had responded by becoming a student of almost incredible industry. It was not unusual for him to spend fifteen consecutive hours over his books. His friend John Page recalled in later years that Jefferson was the only one of their rollicking college group who could turn his back on a good time whenever he chose and retreat for hours of studying. Jefferson's love of books was nothing less than passionate. When his library went up with Shadwell's smoke, he remarked that it was worth 200 pounds - perhaps $5,000 in today's dollars. "I wish it had been the money," he said.

On went the newlyweds, with good wishes from Jefferson's old playmate, "Tuckahoe Tom" Randolph, through a landscape that grew more and more ghostly. Snow was falling in a way it seldom came down in Virginia. The Jeffersons dropped farther and farther behind schedule, and finally the exhausted horses were literally plowing the light phaeton through drifts of three and four feet. Jefferson wisely turned off at Blenheim, one of the numerous Carter estates, seven or eight miles from Monticello.

By now, it was dark, and the snow was falling faster and faster. The newlyweds could have easily taken advantage of the hospitality that was undoubtedly proffered by Blenheim's caretaker. But her husband had fired Martha's imagination with his rhapsodies about his mountain. He could restrain neither her nor himself in their determination to ignore the worst blizzard in decades and push on. On horseback through the driving snow, they slogged to the barely visible road that wound up Monticello's slope.

By now, it was midnight, and on the mountaintop there was not a sign of life. The white workmen and the slaves had long since built up their fires against the howling storm and gone to bed. Trying to heat the few roofed rooms in the half-finished mansion house was out of the question, so Jefferson led Martha to the little one-room cottage he had built in those now laughable days when he pictured himself as the melancholy bachelor hermit, sardonically pondering the ways of the world from his lonely peak.

The place must have been brutally cold. While Martha shivered inside her cloak, the bridegroom constructed a fire with a skill he had learned from his frontiersman father. Soon a roaring blaze sent leaping waves of warmth and light against the walls of their little refuge, turning the wind's howls into a curiously comforting sound. They threw themselves before the blaze and shivered deliciously in each other's arms.

Suddenly, Jefferson leaped up, remembering a hidden treasure. From behind a shelf of books, he flourished with a whoop of triumph a half bottle of wine. Now the evening was complete. With bodies warmed and glasses full, they lolled before the fire like a pair of Indian lovers, Martha's auburn head bent low, her hazel eyes shining over the sketches her husband spread out before her - brilliant promises of the magnificent house in which he vowed they would grow old together.

It was a night they both would remember for the rest of their lives. Neither thought, even for the tiniest moment, that there was anything ominous about that moaning winter wind, keening a kind of dirge around their little island of warmth and happiness. They did not stop to think how precious - and how rare - these moments were for human beings. They were young, life was young, and with such richness in their hearts and on their lips, how could promises fail? Mercifully, the future was as blank as the darkness that shrouded the windows.

2

The great world of Virginia - the courthouses, the plantation mansions - saw nothing of Thomas Jefferson for the next two months. The House of Burgesses met in its red brick capitol at Williamsburg without the young delegate from Albemarle. Fortunately, the county had a second representative, Dr. Thomas Walker, so local needs were not neglected. Even that methodical recorder of Jefferson's goings and comings, his pocket account book, is silent until February 8. Not until April did the Jeffersons end their honeymoon and come down from their mountain for a journey to Williamsburg. They enjoyed the capital's highly social spring season, going to the theater regularly and riding out to visit friends such as the Pages at Rosewell. There was also a more significant visit - to a Dr. Brown. After a month's stopover at The Forest, they rode back to Monticello by easy stages, no longer able to conceal the happy expectation of an addition to the family.

On September 27, 1772, an hour after midnight, Martha gave birth to a daughter, whom Jefferson promptly named after her mother. The baby was underweight and did not seem to thrive. In an era when two out of every three children failed to survive the so-called childhood diseases, this was a bad omen. Someone, perhaps Jefferson, suggested allowing one of the black nurses to lend the baby her breast. The change was miraculous. In a matter of weeks, the little girl was out of danger, and the worried mother and father could smile once more.

Martha recovered very slowly from her pregnancy. On October 20, her father wrote plaintively to Jefferson using the family nickname, which her husband guarded jealously, even from his closest friends: "I have heard nothing about dear Patty since you left this place." It was the first faint hint of future sorrow.

But for a few more months, there was only happiness at Monticello. By now, the basic structure of the mansion was visible. It was organized around a spacious center room with an octagonal end, facing west. Jefferson called this room the parlor, and it was entered from a hall on the east side, through a classic, white-pillared portico. Flanking the parlor was a smaller, square drawing room to the north, balanced by a matching square dining room to the south. These rooms, in turn, opened into small octagonal bow rooms, regaining the motif of the parlor. Off the hall was to be a large staircase to the roomy library above the parlor. Balanced on either side of the library were two bedrooms. Off the parlor, on the west, was another handsome classic portico. The downstairs rooms were eighteen feet high - more than twice the height of the ordinary plantation house. The decorations on the porticos, the mantels, and indoor friezes were carefully selected from the various architectural "orders" – Corinthian, Doric, Ionic. It would, when finally finished, be a house that satisfied both the eye and the mind.

For Martha, perhaps the best proof of her husband's originality was his decision to put all the outbuildings that marred the appearance of so many Virginia plantations below the ground under two L-shaped terraces that were to run from the bow rooms to their honeymoon cottage and another matching cottage on the opposite side of the mountain. There was room underground for everything in Jefferson's ingenious plan: a kitchen, a laundry, a smoke room, a meal room, pantry, and a dairy.

In the summer of 1773, Martha Jefferson was pregnant again. She and everyone else considered it good news. Women had to have a lot of babies if they hoped to raise even a few, and there was little or no thought of childbirth draining a woman's strength by inexorable degrees. Nature and its works were considered beneficent and health giving; women were supposed to blossom during pregnancy.

By now, Jefferson had returned to the practice of law. But politics soon began absorbing more of his time and attention. As a member of the House of Burgesses, he experienced firsthand the prickly relationship gradually developing between the American colonies and the British government. The Burgesses reacted angrily when Parliament announced that henceforth any American who interfered with the operations of the British navy in its attempt to enforce laws against smuggling would be punished by death. Equally infuriating was the edict that the wrongdoer could be transported at the pleasure of His Majesty to any county in England for trial. This was not the first time Parliament indicated that it seemed committed to a policy of deliberately violating rights cherished by Americans in every colony. Agitation against British taxation had been going on since 1765, when young Jefferson, "yet a student of law in Williamsburg," stood in the door of the lobby of the House of Burgesses and heard a backwoods lawyer named Patrick Henry boom a warning that still echoes through American history. "Caesar had his Brutus - Charles I his Cromwell - and George III may profit by their example . . . if *this* be treason, make the most of it."

Jefferson and Henry were close friends in spite of the widest possible divergence in their personalities, habits, and tastes. Jefferson had a classical education and could read Homer in the original Greek and Horace in Latin; he had probed deeply into the roots and foundations of English law for over two years before he began to practice. Henry was almost totally uneducated and had become a lawyer almost on impulse after his country store went bankrupt. He spent no more than six weeks paging through a few elementary textbooks. Jefferson's mentor, scholarly George Wythe, professor of law at William and Mary, was outraged when Henry was admitted to the bar.

Jefferson had first met Henry when they shared the Christmas celebrations at a neighboring plantation the year before Henry's admission to the bar. "His manners had something of the coarseness of the society he had frequented," Jefferson recalled. "His passion was fiddling, dancing, and pleasantry. He excelled in the last, and it attached everyone to him." Although Jefferson was only seventeen at the time and Henry was already a married man, a friendship sprang up that continued through the next decade.

One reason for the friendship, Jefferson said, "was the exact conformity of our political opinions." But equally important to the shy young intellectual was Henry's overwhelming personal charm and oratorical powers. "He appeared to me to speak as Homer wrote," Jefferson said. It was a gift Jefferson himself lacked, but he also saw that oratory was not enough. Henry "could not draw a bill on the most simple subject which would bear legal criticism or even the ordinary criticism which looks to correctness of style and ideas, for indeed there was no accuracy of idea in his head. His imagination was copious, poetical, sublime, but vague also. He said the strongest things in the finest language, but without logic, without arrangement . . ."

In 1773, Jefferson, Henry, Richard Henry Lee, Francis L. Lee, and Dabney Carr, who was in his first term as a burgess, met in a private room at the Raleigh Tavern "to consult on the state of things." They were the young turks in an assembly dominated by older conservative members. They drew up a set of resolutions protesting rumors of parliamentary proceedings "tending to deprive them of their ancient legal and constitutional rights" and moved to create "a standing committee of correspondence and inquiry" to obtain the latest news on such matters from sister colonies.

Jefferson had drawn up the resolutions, but with a generosity that was also a realistic estimate of his oratorical limitations, he suggested that his friend Dabney Carr submit them to the House. Already young Carr, practicing law in the same courts with Patrick Henry, had proven himself a formidable rival to Henry. Jefferson was eager to give his friend a chance to display his talents in the political arena. Carr performed magnificently, and the motions passed without a dissenting vote. The royal governor, the Earl of Dunmore, promptly dissolved the House, indicating his august disapproval, but Jefferson and his friends, undaunted, retreated to the tavern, and the Committee of Correspondence began functioning the very next day.

Jefferson and Carr returned to Albemarle for the same reason: Their wives were pregnant, Carr's for the sixth time. There, on May 16, 1773, just thirty-five days after his brilliant debut in the House of Burgesses, Dabney Carr died in Charlottesville of "bilious fever" - a term doctors used in those days to describe a disease they could not identify. The illness was so swift and violent neither Jefferson, who seems to have been away on business, nor Mrs. Carr, just recovering from childbirth, reached him before he expired.

When Jefferson returned home to hear the sorrowful news, Carr was already buried at Shadwell. Sadly, Jefferson remembered their boyhood promise and ordered some workmen to set out a graveyard beneath the great oak, where he and Dabney had spent so many happy hours. A few days later, the best friend of his Albemarle youth was reinterred there, and Jefferson himself wrote his epitaph, making clear that it was a tribute from "Thomas

Jefferson, who of all men living loved him most." Jefferson and Martha opened their doors to Carr's widow and six children. Henceforth, Jefferson declared, he would regard the children as his own.

Two weeks later came more grim news. John Wayles was dead at The Forest. Martha's father was fifty-eight. His passing did not cause the kind of pain aroused by the death of Dabney Carr, but it meant a great deal more responsibility for Jefferson and his wife. The following year, when the estate was settled, they acquired more than 11,000 additional acres of land and 142 slaves, doubling the land and number of slaves they already owned. Unfortunately, the property came encumbered with a heavy debt - over 3,000 pounds - to British merchants.

This was a nagging problem, not easily solved because even when Jefferson sold 6,000 acres of Martha's land to pay it off, he could get only bonds - promissory notes - from his fellow Virginians, and the English creditors refused to accept them. However, this was not an immediate worry. More to the point was the rather overwhelming task of running this vast estate and simultaneously practicing law and politics.

Far from being trained to business, Martha was, if anything, completely dependent on Jefferson for almost every decision, and running a half dozen farms with nearly 200 slaves and several dozen white overseers and skilled workmen required decisions constantly. She was also dependent in another sense. She lamented every day Jefferson spent away from her - and as a lawyer, he was inevitably forced to practice at distant county courthouses, as well as at Williamsburg.

At the same time, Jefferson was becoming disillusioned with the law. His $3,000 income was on paper. He rarely managed to collect more than half his fees from his cash-short clients. Letting bills glide on for years was an old Virginia tradition. In August 1774, he turned over his entire practice to twenty-one-year-old Edmund Randolph, son of John Randolph, the attorney general of Virginia, listing 132 active cases and surrendering to his cousin two-thirds of the prospective fees.

Jefferson's tobacco fields still earned him a solid income. He added to his library and his wine cellar, pushed ahead on the construction of his house, and picked up bits of land that interested him. In 1773, he exulted over the purchase of 120 acres in Bedford County, containing a unique piece of architecture today called the Natural Bridge. As a true son of Peter Jefferson, he had climbed to the top of this remarkable relic of another geological age. Here, his nerve failed him, and he yielded to the usual human reaction to that dizzying view. "You involuntarily fall on your hands and feet and creep to the parapet and peep over it," he wrote. "Looking down from this height for about a minute gave me a violent headache." If Jefferson found the view from the top "painful and intolerable," from below, he found it "delightful in an equal extreme. It is impossible for the emotions arising from the sublime to be felt beyond what they are here; so beautiful an arch, so elevated, so light, and springing as it were up to heaven, the rapture of the spectator is really indescribable."

As Martha's pregnancy advanced, Jefferson spent more and more time at home. He cut winding paths that he called roundabouts through Monticello's forested slopes. Ultimately he had four of these for woodland wandering, connecting them by oblique roads. He planted fruit trees and a vegetable garden on the southeastern slope. In his garden book, these vegetables suddenly began to blossom with exotic names: *aglio di Toscania* for garlic, *radicchio di Pistoia* for endive. The Italian names are the first evidence of Monticello's new neighbor, the Italian physician and political philosopher, Philip Mazzei. Banished from Italy for his revolutionary thinking, Mazzei had prospered as a wine merchant in London for a number of years. He had come to Virginia to plant vineyards and start a local wine industry and was en route to the Shenandoah Valley, where his patron and traveling companion, the London merchant Thomas Adams, had property. The two men stopped overnight at Monticello. The household was asleep, but in the dawn, Jefferson arose and greeted Mazzei, whom he took on a long walk around the neighborhood.

Mazzei found himself amazed by the ease with which Jefferson discussed science, literature, politics, and religion. Before the Italian knew what was happening, he was letting Jefferson persuade him to buy 400 acres of land adjoining Monticello to which Jefferson generously added 2,000 acres of his own land. Returning to Monticello for breakfast, they greeted Thomas Adams with obviously conspiratorial looks. "I see by your expression that you've taken him away from me," sighed Adams. "I knew you would do that."

In a matter of days, Jefferson had Mazzei's men and equipment transported to Monticello. The workmen, who had not heard a word of their native tongue since leaving Italy, burst into tears of joy when Jefferson greeted them in Italian - a language he had never heard spoken until he met Mazzei, but which he had taught himself to read fluently in his student days. Mazzei settled down to become an almost too fervent admirer. There were times when his nonstop conversation left Jefferson, no mean talker himself, wondering if the good doctor would ever run down.

By and large, Jefferson was delighted with the success of his first venture into international friendship, and both he and Martha enjoyed the zest that the volatile Latin added to Monticello's Anglo-Saxon atmosphere. All they needed now, the Jeffersons fervently agreed, was a son. As Martha's second pregnancy reached its term in the spring of 1774, their hopes were high. But Martha gave birth to another daughter, whom they named Jane Randolph after Jefferson's mother. Again, Martha's recovery from the ordeal was slow. It was obvious that for her, pregnancy was both an emotional and physical crisis. Her own mother had died in childbirth, and the memory was a perpetual threat to her peace of mind.

But Martha's very fragility only made her husband love her all the more. He nursed and fussed over her, and pronounced himself still the happiest of men. Two children safely born, his mansion growing daily before his eyes, a cultured neighbor to add some social spice to their daily round - life seemed quintessentially happy to Jefferson in that spring of 1774. He played with "Patsy," his private name for little Martha, toddling now at eighteen months, and began personally supervising the education of young Peter Carr, Dabney's oldest son. Together he and Martha worked in the vegetable garden. In the evening, they would read aloud to each other - perhaps *Tristram Shandy* or Jefferson's other favorite, *The Poems of Ossian*, "translated" by James Macpherson. These were supposed to be the works of a Celtic Homer who flourished in the dawn of Scotch-Irish history, discovered by the learned Macpherson in the Scottish Highlands.

The Jeffersons, like thousands of other eighteenth-century readers, did not realize they were victims

of one of the great literary hoaxes of all time.
Macpherson had created Ossian in his own
romantic imagination and when the poems became
sensationally successful, did not have the nerve
to admit that he, a failure as a poet under his own
byline, was the actual author. Real or fake, the
poems reveal the deeply romantic side of Jefferson's
complex mind. Among the favorite passages heard
before the firelight in Monticello's parlor was this
one from "The Songs of Selma."

Star of descending night!

Fair is thy light in the west!

Thou liftest thy unshorn head from thy
cloud:

Thy steps are stately on thy hill.

What dost thou behold in the plain?

The stormy winds are laid.

The murmur of the torrent comes from afar.

Roaring waves climb the distant rock.

The flies of evening are on their feeble wings;

The hum of their course is on the field.

What dost thou behold, fair light?

But thou dost smile and depart.

The waves come with joy around thee:

They bathe thy lovely hair.

Farewell, thou silent beam!

Let the light of Ossian's soul arise!

On Monticello's peak, Jefferson's mind soared off in every direction. The hours became an almost continuous enjoyment of beauty in books, in the woman he loved and the children she had given him, and in the bountiful, blooming world of nature that fascinated both his eye and his mind. It is easy to see how this scholarly, reflective man began to treasure every hour he lived on this mountain and willingly would have spent the rest of his life there, yielding with reluctance the few days a year he was required to sit in the House of Burgesses.

But beyond the horizon of the world that Jefferson commanded from his hilltop, events were about to force him to surrender that dream. Three and a half months before Jane Randolph Jefferson was born, a group of Bostonians disguised as Indians dumped 342 chests of British tea into the murky waters of the harbor to underscore their refusal to pay the tax Parliament had placed on this favorite American brew. On April 22, another group of "Indians" performed a similar dumping operation in New York harbor.

An angry Parliament retaliated by closing the port

of Boston and ramming through a series of acts that all but annulled the Massachusetts charter.

None of this bad news had reached Jefferson or his fellow burgesses when they assembled in Williamsburg on May 5, 1774, in response to the summons of Governor Dunmore. On May 22, dust-covered express riders from the Boston Committee of Correspondence came pounding into the colonial capital with the news of Parliament's overbearing retaliation and a call from Massachusetts for aid from her sister colonies.

Jefferson, Patrick Henry, Edmund Randolph, and the other young turks met in a private caucus to decide how to seize the political initiative and persuade the older conservatives to join in a public statement of solidarity with Massachusetts. Flowery resolutions would never win a majority vote, no matter how thunderingly Patrick Henry supported them. For the past two years, the people had been showing obvious signs of boredom with political fulminations. The colony was in a kind of "lethargy . . . as to passing events," Jefferson later recalled.

For the first time, Jefferson revealed the intuitive judgment of the born political leader. The only thing that was likely to "alarm" the popular attention, he told Henry and the others, was a day of general fasting and prayer. Not since 1755, during a war with France, had "such a solemnity" been invoked. The beauty of the idea was instantly apparent.

The group spent the rest of the night rummaging through old forms and proclamations and, in Jefferson's words, "we cooked up a resolution . . . for a day of fasting, humiliation, and prayer to implore heaven to avert from us the evils of civil war, to inspire us with firmness in support of our rights, and to turn the hearts of the King and Parliament to moderation and justice." The next day, the self-appointed revolutionary committee went to Robert Carter Nicholas, treasurer of the colony and one of the gravest and most religious members of the House of Burgesses, and asked him to introduce the resolution. It passed without a single dissenting vote, and Lord Dunmore immediately dissolved the assembly.

Now it was easy for Jefferson and his fellow firebrands to lead a march to the Raleigh Tavern, where eighty-nine burgesses agreed to form a permanent association and ordered the Committee of Correspondence to inform committees in other colonies about Virginia's day of fast. The association also declared "that an attack made on one of our sister colonies is an attack made on all British America and threatens ruin to the rights of all." Most important was the call for all the colonies to meet in congress "at such place, annually, as should be convenient to direct from time to time the measures required by the general interest."

Jefferson did not stay in Williamsburg to march

with his fellow burgesses to Bruton Church on June 1. He hurried home to Monticello and Martha. But he arranged for church services in his native Albemarle County and years later he recalled how "the effect of the day, through the whole colony, was like a shock of electricity, arousing every man and placing him erect and solidly on his center."

In August, Jefferson was back in Williamsburg, as Albemarle's representative at a "convention" of delegates that Lord Dunmore could not dissolve with a stroke of his royal pen. The county nominated Jefferson and John Walker, Jefferson's neighbor and former classmate, to act for them at this meeting, and the freeholders of the county also approved a series of resolutions that Jefferson had written. They called on Americans to stand fast against Parliament's invasion of their rights and asserted that "no other legislature whatever" could exercise authority over Americans but those "duly constituted and appointed with their own consent" - the colonial assemblies. The resolutions also urged a boycott of all commodities on which Parliament placed a tax and demanded the repeal of parliamentary laws that blocked the growth of American manufacturing and restricted American trade. These ideas were far bolder than anything that emanated from other local Virginia conventions. The freeholders of Hanover County, Patrick Henry's bailiwick, only demanded "the privileges and immunities of their fellow subjects in England" and asked that they be permitted "to continue to live under the genuine unaltered constitution of England and be subjects in the true spirit of that constitution to His Majesty and his illustrious house." Burgess George Washington's Fairfax County conceded the right of Parliament to regulate American trade and commerce. "Such a power directed with wisdom and moderation seems necessary for the general good of that great body politic of which we are a part . . . Under this idea our ancestors submitted to it."

But Jefferson was prepared to be even bolder. He expanded the Albemarle resolutions into a vivid essay that he planned to submit to the Williamsburg convention as a "declaration of rights." This bristling document, twenty-three printed pages long, set forth Jefferson's contention that the colonists were subject to no laws but those of their own creation. "Our emigration from England to this country," he said, "gave her no more rights over us than the emigrations of the Danes and Saxons gave to the present authorities of the mother country over England." This was the legal scholar Jefferson speaking, and it did not in the least trouble him that he knew only one man who agreed with him - his old law-school mentor, George Wythe.

The declaration went on to denounce the "arbitrary measures" of both king and Parliament and condemned even more vigorously the use of "large bodies of armed forces not made up of the people here nor raised by the authority of our laws" to enforce them. "His Majesty has no right to land a single armed man on our shores," Jefferson declared. Finally, defending his bold tone, Jefferson said that "freedom of language and sentiment . . . becomes a free people, claiming their rights as derived from the laws of nature, not as the gift of their chief magistrate. Let those flatter who fear: it is not an American art."

This was more than bold; it was outrageously daring. In an age when kings were still approached with scraping bows and humble petitions, Jefferson lectured the British sovereign, head of a global empire that ranged from America through the West Indies to India. "Open your breast, Sire, to liberal and expanded thought. Let not the name of George III be a blot in the page of history."

Jefferson never got a chance to submit personally these burning words to the Virginia convention. On the road to Williamsburg, he was stricken with an attack of dysentery and was forced to retreat to Monticello. He forwarded two copies of the declaration - one to Patrick Henry and the other to his cousin Peyton Randolph, slated to be the chairman of the convention.

The copy sent to Henry vanished into the silence. "Whether Mr. Henry disapproved the ground taken or was too lazy to read it (for he was the laziest man in reading I ever knew), I never learned," Jefferson wrote later, "but he communicated it to nobody." Peyton Randolph laid the essay on the table for other members to read. The conservative majority thought it was "too bold for the present state of things." But Jefferson's friends in the convention, without bothering to ask his permission, had it printed in Williamsburg as "A Summary View of the Rights of British America." No doubt thinking to protect him, they did not list Jefferson by name as the author but simply said the pamphlet was "by a native and member of the House of Burgesses." The essay made its way to England where it was soon reprinted by Britishers sympathetic to the American cause.

Virginia's call for a continental congress had won a prompt response from Massachusetts, and other colonies quickly joined in a plan to gather in Philadelphia. The Virginia convention chose seven delegates to this momentous meeting. They included Peyton Randolph, who exuded integrity and dignity; Benjamin Harrison V, whose son, William Henry Harrison, and great-grandson, Benjamin Harrison, would later become U.S. presidents; the firebrand Patrick Henry; and Colonel George Washington, the colony's most distinguished soldier. These men were all a decade or more older than Jefferson. However ample the evidence of Jefferson's maturity as a writer, he was a comparative newcomer to the Virginia establishment, and in no sense an acknowledged leader or persuader of men, such as Colonel Washington or Patrick Henry.

This fact did not disturb Jefferson in the least. He had no great desire to endure the long journey to Philadelphia, and the weeks, perhaps months, of separation from Martha that it would inevitably involve. He was perfectly content to be a distant spectator to the first congress and its decisions, which more or less followed the policy spelled out by the Virginia convention.

The fifty-six delegates from twelve colonies issued a series of declarations that set forth the rights of the colonists, among them "life, liberty, and property." They named thirteen parliamentary acts since 1763 that violated American rights and denounced particularly the so-called "coercive acts" against Massachusetts. Finally, they formed a continental association pledged to cease all imports from Great Britain after December 1. They also placed an embargo on all exports to Britain, Ireland, and the West Indies beginning September 1, 1775. Then, with a conciliatory address to the king and the British and American peoples, congress adjourned but resolved to meet again on May 10, 1775, if the crisis between the colonies and the mother country continued.

Jefferson wholeheartedly supported the nonimportation agreement, joining the association and persuading friends and relatives to sign up as well. In fact, he was so scrupulous he offered to destroy a shipment of sash windows that he had ordered from England before the association was created. The Committee of Safety at Norfolk was more lenient toward the author of "A Summary Declaration" than he was disposed to be toward himself, and permitted the forbidden window frames to proceed safely to their destination at Monticello. Harrison was one committeeman inclined to make exceptions in deserving cases.

Events moved slowly in the eighteenth century, especially when the main actors were separated by 3,000 miles of ocean. For the next several months, Jefferson stayed at Monticello pushing the work on his mansion house. Everything - nails, timber, bricks - had to be fabricated on the plantation and most of the skilled labor had to be trained on the job. How closely Jefferson supervised the work can be seen from his voluminous notebooks. He calculated precisely how many bricks he needed for the various parts of the house: "NE walls and partitions of parlor 77½F. in length, to raise the story, 82,000 bricks. SE walls to raise the story, 40,000, whole, to raise second story, 63,000." Fifty thousand bricks were burned and laid in 1774 alone. By the end of the year, Jefferson had completed what he called "the middle building" containing the parlor, library, drawing room, and bedroom above it.

The well-trained Martha tried her utmost to

please her methodical husband by keeping careful records in her domain. On the back of some of Jefferson's legal papers, in a beautifully delicate script, she wrote:

> February 10th. Opened a barrel of Col. Harrison's flour
>
> 13 A mutton killed
>
> 17 Two pullets killed
>
> 27 A cask of small beer brewed, 15 gallon cask

She inventoried her house linens too. Early in her marriage she counted:

> 6 diaper tablecloths, 10 ditto damask
>
> 12 diaper napkins marked TJ 71
>
> 12 ditto towels, TJ 71
>
> 6 pr. sheets, 15 pillow cases, TJ 71

Next came "a list of our clothes." Jefferson had:

> 9 ruffled shirts and 18 plain ditto
>
> 20 old cambrick stocks
>
> 15 old rags of pocket handkerchieves
>
> 3 pr. of English Cordied breeches
>
> 4 of Virginia ditto

6 Virginia cordied dimitied waistcoats

13 pair white silk stockings

5 red waistcoats, 2 buff, 1 white flannel ditto
1 green coat

1 black princes ditto

Among her own clothes she listed:

16 old shifts, 4 new ditto

6 old fine aprons

4 Virginia pettycoats

9 pr of silk stockings, 10 pr of old cotton 8
silk gowns

6 washing ditto old and 2 new to make up

2 suits of Brussels lace, 1 suit of worked
muslin

On went the lists, noting the consumption of a goose, the slaughter of a beef cow, the eating of six hams and four shoulders. Beside these facts, Martha Jefferson's pen would pause and sketch solemn little birds perched on leafy twigs. Obviously, Martha yearned to escape such a dull routine - and it is easy to picture her doing just that, with a husband who was both doting and energetic. Always up before the sun, Jefferson had no trouble absorbing into his own hands all the business of the plantation, from the minute details of interior decoration (he even designed the curtains and chose the fabric) down to selecting the meat for the next day's dinner.

Elsewhere in Virginia, life continued its peaceful, pleasant flow. Philip Fithian, a young New Jersey clergyman who was tutoring the children of Robert Carter at Nomminy Hall on the James, told of going to visit the nearby Lee plantation for a typical ball. The dinner, he reported, "was as elegant as could be well expected when so great an Assembly were to be kept for so long a time. For drink, there were several sorts of wine, good lemon punch, toddy, cyder, porter &c." The young Presbyterian clergyman watched the ladies and gentlemen dancing in the ballroom, and he noted how, when dancing, the ladies' "silks and brocades rustled and trailed behind them." He also noted that the men, in the privacy of the card rooms, were "toasting the sons of America; some singing 'liberty songs' as they called them, in which six, eight, ten or more would put their heads near together and roar . . ."

Like all Virginians, Jefferson kept in close touch with the political situation through the Virginia *Gazette,* and there he read in early February the report of the ominous speech that George III had made at the opening of Parliament. The king had grimly declared that he was determined to uphold "Parliament's supreme authority." The minority who tried to speak on behalf of the embattled

Americans were ruthlessly voted down. The *Gazette* also reported a few weeks later that the king had received without comment the conciliatory petition of the Continental Congress.

In the middle of March 1775, Jefferson departed Monticello to still another Virginia convention, this time held in Richmond to make sure that the colony's royal governor, Lord Dunmore, made no attempt to interfere with it. The governor was growing increasingly restive about the almost total dissolution of his authority. En route to Richmond, Jefferson left Martha and the two girls at Elk Hill, one of the plantations they had inherited from John Wayles. The problems of caring for two small children in Monticello's unfinished mansion were obviously many, and Jefferson felt Martha would be far more comfortable, as well as nearer to him, at this fine old house overlooking a fertile island in the peaceful James.

The Virginia convention, largely the same delegates who had formed the previous one, met in white-walled St. John's Church in Richmond. Jefferson, Patrick Henry, Richard Henry Lee, and the other young men were astonished to discover that in spite of the king's speech, a majority were against any and all measures that might tend to arouse popular emotions. After approving by unanimous vote the resolutions of the Continental Congress, the delegates sat back and listened to a petition to the king by the Jamaican assembly, supporting American rights. The mood of the majority was reflected in the resolution of thanks they forwarded to Jamaica, assuring the islanders that it was "the most ardent wish of this colony . . . to see a speedy return of those halcyon days, when we lived a free and happy people." Obviously, most of the delegates were inclined to believe that a blizzard of respectful petitions from colonies around the world would change His Majesty's mind and persuade him to take back the dour words he had spoken to Parliament. This mood of moderate optimism was exploded by Patrick Henry.

Grimly, the Hanover County orator, still self-consciously wearing his backwoods homespun in contrast to the satin and superfine broadcloth of the majority of the delegates, rose to introduce a call for an independent militia to put Virginia "into a posture of defense." Richard Henry Lee, a debater not quite as thunderous as Henry (Jefferson called him "frothy and rhetorical") but effective nonetheless, rose to second the resolution. Emphatically, the established leaders rose one by one to denounce the militia resolution. They insisted the king was showing signs of relenting, and they questioned the wisdom of committing what could be construed by the British as an act of war. They reminded Henry that it was imperial Britain he was daring, an empire with an army and fleet second to none in the world.

Henry rose magnificently to the oratorical challenge. He insisted war was inevitable. The king, far from seeking reconciliation, was already using "the implements of war and subjugation" - armies and fleets – [to] cow Americans into surrender without a fight. "If we wish to be free - if we mean to preserve inviolate these inestimable privileges for which we have been so long contending . . . we must fight! I repeat it, sir, we must fight!"

In the First Continental Congress, Henry had declared he was no longer a Virginian but an American. Now he used the idea to scoff at the argument that Virginia was too weak. It wasn't true if Virginia considered herself part of an American union. "Three millions of people armed in the holy cause of liberty and in such a country as that which we possess are invincible by any force which our enemy can send against us," he thundered. ". . . the battle, sir, is not to the strong alone; it is to the vigilant, the active, the brave . . . I know not what course others may take, but as for me, give me liberty or give me death!"

Contrary to popular myth, Henry's speech by no means silenced the opposition. The debate raged on, and Jefferson, as one of Henry's backers, made one of the few public speeches of his career, arguing "closely, profoundly and warmly" on behalf of preparedness.

Finally, by a very close vote, the assembly agreed to appoint a militia committee to reorganize Virginia's armed forces. Jefferson was named a member of the twelve-man committee that recommended that each county raise at least one sixty-eight-man company of infantry and one thirty-man troop of cavalry and see that both were trained and equipped with ammunition and weapons, including that native American invention, the tomahawk. This was hardly a formidable fighting force even if all the companies could have been assembled quickly, which in a colony Virginia's size was clearly impossible. For all of Henry's bold words, the committee obviously, as Jefferson said in later years, "slackened our pace that our less ardent colleagues might keep up with us."

After approving this mild defensive posture, the delegates reelected the same men to represent them at the second meeting of the Continental Congress in Philadelphia. Almost as an afterthought, Jefferson was elected as an alternate, in case Governor Dunmore called a meeting of the House of Burgesses and the delegation's leader, Peyton Randolph, was forced to return to Virginia to preside over this body.

Jefferson gathered his wife and two daughters from Elk Hill and returned to Monticello, where he plunged once more into his little world of building and farming. In distant Massachusetts, the appeal to arms that Patrick Henry had declared inevitable became bloody reality when militiamen clashed with British regulars on Lexington green and at Concord bridge and drove the startled British back to Boston in a day-long running battle.

Even before this news reached Virginia, the colony was aroused by a very rash move on the part of Lord Dunmore. On the moonlit night of April 20, Dunmore persuaded the captain of a British revenue cutter, the *Magdalene,* to spirit twenty barrels of powder out of the Williamsburg magazine. He was caught in the act, and the entire colony rose in wrath against him. Patrick Henry placed himself at the head of the militia from Hanover County and began marching for Williamsburg.

While the colony seethed, express riders from Massachusetts arrived with the news of Lexington. At Monticello, Jefferson heard it early in May. No matter how deeply he was committed to defending American rights, the bloodshed filled him with dismay, and it made him sad to think that Parliament's folly might separate him from friends and loyalties that had for years been part of his life.

On May 7, he wrote a touching letter to his old William and Mary professor, William Small, who was living in England. He sent Small three dozen bottles of Madeira, "half of a present which I had laid by for you." Then he grimly recited the bloody news from Massachusetts. Others were denouncing it as British barbarism, but Jefferson called it "this accident" that "has cut off our last hope of reconciliation." After several more lines on the disintegrating relations between the colonies and the mother country, Jefferson broke off: "But I am getting into politics though I sat down only to ask your acceptance of the wine and express my constant wishes for your happiness." He was no war lover, this Jefferson.

On June 1, Jefferson was on his way to Williamsburg again in his durable phaeton. Governor Dunmore, for want of a better idea, had called a meeting of the House of Burgesses. Peyton Randolph hurried back to take his seat as speaker, and under his leadership, the burgesses pressed the question of the stolen gunpowder so angrily that Dunmore panicked and retreated with his wife and family to the man-of-war *Fowey* off Yorktown. Peyton Randolph, meanwhile, showed the growing reliance of the older generation on young Jefferson's literary skills by asking him to draft a reply to the governor's message, calling on the assembly to consider the "alarming situation of the country."

Jefferson composed a masterful document, calm and moderate in tone but unbending in spirit.

Significant was the clear declaration that the reply was offered "only as an individual part of the whole empire. Final determination we leave to the general Congress now sitting . . . To them also we refer the discovery of that proper method of representing our well-founded grievances . . . For ourselves, we have exhausted every mode of application which our invention could suggest as proper and promising."

With Governor Dunmore all but abandoning the colony, the Virginians decided to stay in session and provide the state with a central government. This meant Peyton Randolph had to remain in Williamsburg. While one of the moderates, Archibald Cary, read Jefferson's coolly chiseled reply to Lord Dunmore's empty chair in the House of Burgesses, Jefferson jolted north in his phaeton toward Philadelphia and a rendezvous with world history. He went as a man deeply troubled about the state of his world and - equally important to him - with a nagging fear in the back of his mind that his wife was not strong enough to handle the heavy responsibilities he was leaving behind him. The mere fact of his absence would be a burden she had never borne easily - and now she had the added worry of seeing him involved in what looked more and more like a civil war.

3

The Philadelphia into which Jefferson rode after a leisurely ten-day journey was not an entirely new world to him. He had visited it ten years before, in 1765, to be inoculated for smallpox. But it was, nevertheless, a sharp contrast to the Virginia world he knew best. Williamsburg, with its population of 2,000, was a village compared with this metropolis with paved and lighted streets and 34,000 inhabitants pursuing a dazzling variety of trades and professions. Moreover, the city was in the process of being transformed into an armed camp. Philadelphia Associaters, Quaker Blues - all sorts of companies - drilled and practiced in factory yards and open fields. If Lexington was not yet a shot heard around the world, it had certainly echoed up and down the continent of North America.

The second Congress had already been in session six weeks when Jefferson arrived. Delegates were sitting in the red brick colonial State House, sixty-five men from all thirteen of the colonies, although the member from Georgia was only a quasi-official personage. Virginia's substitute delegate quartered his horses with Jacob Hiltzheimer and found rooms with a cabinetmaker named Benjamin Randolph. That night, Jefferson ate at the City Tavern with the Virginia delegates and a scattering of delegates from other colonies.

The next morning, June 22, 1775, he presented his credentials to Congress and was seated as a duly-certified member. His architect's eye undoubtedly appreciated the graceful proportion of the State House's white-paneled ground-floor chamber, lined on two sides with windows and surmounted by a handsome glass prism chandelier in the center. The heat of the room, with the doors and most of the windows closed to guarantee the secrecy of the deliberations, did not bother a Virginian as much as it wilted the New Yorkers and New Englanders.

Jefferson had already heard from his fellow delegates some shrewd estimates of the leaders from other states - the chief liberty men from Massachusetts, Samuel Adams, with his palsied hands and quavering voice, and his cousin, John Adams, learned in legal history and sharp tongued in debate; witty Caesar Rodney of Pennsylvania; fiery Christopher Gadsen of South Carolina and the Rutledge brothers from the same state, strutting cavaliers. But the man Jefferson's eyes sought first was a newcomer to the Pennsylvania delegation - Benjamin Franklin, home from almost a decade in England where he had been America's spokesman. In his plain brown suit, the gray hair falling on his shoulders, the old man was a model of philosophic moderation.

Jefferson by no means slipped into Congress unnoticed or unheralded. He brought with him from Virginia the colony's reply to Parliament's so-called conciliatory proposals. The Old Dominion was the first of the colonies to answer this attempt to divide them, and Jefferson's firm, unbending tone and well-tempered prose had a heartening impact on the weary delegates. Congress seemed to be getting nowhere. A moderate faction, led by wealthy John Dickinson of Pennsylvania, had clashed violently with the coalition of New Englanders and southerners who were in favor of a defiant stand. Over fierce protests from John Adams, Congress had voted unanimously to give Dickinson his way and present another humble petition to the king.

Shrewd politicking on the part of the Adamses had, it was true, produced one step forward. John Adams had nominated Virginia's favorite soldier, George Washington, to take command of the army of New Englanders besieging the British on the outskirts of Boston. The next day, Friday, June 23, Jefferson probably rode out with most of the Congress when the new general departed. It was a festive, highly martial occasion - the Philadelphia Light Horse in white breeches and gleaming high-topped boots riding escort, and men, women, and children lining the roads to give resounding cheers to the big Virginian who never looked more like a leader of men than when he was sitting on a horse.

Little more than three hours after Washington had departed, a far less glittering horseman came thumping into Philadelphia with more bloody news from Massachusetts. On June 17, the very day Congress had chosen Washington to be general-in-chief, militiamen from Massachusetts, Connecticut, Rhode Island, and New Hampshire had fought a stupendous battle with the best of the British army. The British regulars had attacked the Americans in fortifications that had been erected on Breed's and Bunker's hill, part of a neck of land known as Charlestown Heights, overlooking the city of Boston. Bunker Hill was no running skirmish, begun by some headstrong soldier's itchy trigger finger, as at Lexington, but a battle as formal and fierce as any fought against France, in Canada, or in Europe. Four hundred Americans were dead or wounded. Twice, perhaps three times that number of attacking British regulars had fallen before the steadier guns of the American defenders. In Charlestown, across the harbor from Boston, perhaps 300 fine houses had been burned to the ground by hot shot fired from

British warships. The Americans had been driven out of their entrenchments, but they had fallen back to their siege lines around Boston and were priming their guns for another British assault. This action, Jefferson told his brother-in-law Francis Eppes two days later, meant "that the war is now heartily entered into, without a prospect of accommodation . . ."

The news jolted Congress into action. The next day, a committee that had been appointed to prepare a declaration on the causes of taking up arms submitted a paper written by John Rutledge of South Carolina. The paper drew much critical fire. On June 26, it was recommitted, and Jefferson and John Dickinson were added to the committee. When Congress adjourned that day, Jefferson approached another member of the committee, William Livingston of New York, and suggested that Livingston do a draft of a revision. Livingston promptly excused himself and urged instead that Jefferson do it. Jefferson insisted Livingston was the better man.

"We are as yet but new acquaintances, sir," said Livingston. "Why are you so earnest for my doing it?"

"Because," said Jefferson, "I have been informed that you drew the address to the people of Great Britain, a production certainly of the finest pen in America."

"On that," Livingston said, "perhaps, sir, you may not have been correctly informed," and went on to explain that thirty-year-old John Jay of New York, the only delegate younger than Jefferson, had done the writing.

The other member of the committee that drew up this final document of the first Congress had been Richard Henry Lee. The next morning, Jefferson discovered firsthand the animosities that were taking root beneath the general air of unanimity. He saw Jay speaking vehemently to Lee, and then "leading him by the button of his coat" to confront Jefferson. "I understand, sir," said Jay, "that this gentleman informed you that Governor Livingston drew the address to the people of Great Britain."

The mortified Jefferson had to hastily assure him that he had received the information from another Virginian, not Lee. He vowed that "not a word had ever passed on the subject" between him and Lee.

The subject was dropped, but Jefferson had discovered the hard way what John Adams was writing home. Each delegate considered himself "a great man, an orator, a critic, a statesman" and was intensely concerned about his imaginary reputation. This natural hostility had been accentuated by what Jefferson called "some sparrings in debate" between the radical Lee and the moderate Jay.

In this acrimonious atmosphere, Jefferson displayed for the first time another political gift - an ability to win and hold the friendship of remarkably opposite men without compromising his own principles. Contentious John Adams wrote later that Jefferson "though a silent member in Congress . . . was so prompt, frank, explicit and decisive upon committees and in conversation - not even Samuel Adams was more so - that he soon seized upon my heart." But Jefferson was equally friendly with jolly Benjamin Harrison V, whom the stiff-necked Adams described as "another Sir John Falstaff . . . his conversation disgusting to every man of delicacy or decorum."

During his first weeks in the Continental Congress, Jefferson demonstrated this tolerant spirit to an extraordinary degree. His draft of the declaration of the causes of taking up arms was strongly criticized by John Dickinson. "He still retained the hope of reconciliation with the mother country," Jefferson recalled later, "and was unwilling it should be lessened by offensive statements. He was so honest a man and so able a one that he was greatly indulged, even by those who could not feel his scruples. We therefore requested him to take the paper and put it into a form he could approve. He did so, preparing an entire new statement and preserving of the former only the last four paragraphs and half of the preceding one. We approved and reported it to Congress, who accepted it."

Here, Jefferson learned a valuable political

lesson - the power of a single individual to persuade intelligent men to vote against their inclinations. "Congress gave a signal proof of their indulgence of Mr. Dickinson . . . by permitting him to draw their second petition to the King according to his own ideas, and passing it with scarcely any amendment. The disgust against this humility was general, and Mr. Dickinson's delight at its passage was the only circumstance which reconciled them to it." Also involved was the lesson Thomas Jefferson had already learned in Virginia - the necessity "not to go too fast for any respectable part of our body."

But there was no doubt that Jefferson glowed with carefully concealed delight when Dickinson, rising to express his satisfaction with the approval of his petition, said, "There is but one word, Mr. President, in the paper which I disapprove, and that is the word Congress." Up from his chair heaved Harrison to drawl, "There is but one word in the paper, Mr. President, of which I approve, and that is the word Congress."

In a letter to Massachusetts, John Adams denounced the humble petition. "Puerilities become not a great assembly like this the representative of a great people." Finally, he unleashed a personal shaft at Dickinson. "A certain great fortune and piddling genius whose fame has been trumpeted so loudly, has given a silly cast to our whole doings."

The letter was captured by the British and

published, converting Dickinson into one of Adams's permanent enemies. In contrast, Jefferson refused to let the wranglings and dawdlings of Congress disturb his essentially even disposition. He declined to enter the debates and became almost as famous for his silence as Patrick Henry and John Adams for their oratory. But in the long afternoon and evening hours of discussion with the fellow members of his committee and with other congressmen at breakfasts and dinners, he continued to be the "prompt, frank, explicit and decisive" spokesman of a tough though not yet revolutionary stand.

Writing to the Virginia convention on behalf of his fellow delegates, Jefferson said, "The present crisis is so full of danger and incertainty that opinions here are various." He went on to urge the convention to "reflect on the propriety of being prepared for the worst events and . . . to be guarded against probable evils at least" by doing everything in their power to achieve a respectable military posture. Jefferson once more demonstrated that, though no war lover, he was a realist. His study of history had made it clear to him that force was the only answer to those who tried to impose their politics at the point of a gun.

Jefferson's colleagues soon demonstrated that they still valued his pen by making him a member of a committee to draw up an answer to Lord North's so-called "Conciliatory Proposal." The other members were Benjamin Franklin, John Adams, and Richard Henry Lee. Even the prestigious Franklin was sufficiently impressed with the reply Jefferson had written for the Virginia convention to ask him to do the writing.

On July 31, 1775, Congress unanimously approved Jefferson's reply on their behalf to Lord North. The document substantially followed the one he had written for Virginia, but the tone was cooler and more dispassionate. Jefferson aimed at a more lofty dignity, befitting a continental congress. But the carefully controlled anger against British injustice could be seen smoldering beneath individual sentences such as, "We do not mean that our people shall be burthened (burdened) with oppressive taxes, to provide cynosures for the idle or the wicked, under color of providing for a civil list."

In the conclusion, Jefferson achieved a sonorous, almost majestic defiance. "When it [the world] considers the great armaments with which they have invaded us and the circumstances of cruelty with which these have commenced and prosecuted hostilities; when things we say are laid together and attentively considered, can the world be deceived into an opinion that we are unreasonable, or can it hesitate to believe with us that nothing but our own exertions may defeat the ministerial sentence of death or abject submission?"

Two days later, Congress adjourned. It really had

no choice since more than a few of the exhausted delegates had already departed and the Virginia delegation had announced they planned to follow. Benjamin Harrison had wryly remarked, "I think it is high time there was an end of it. We have been too long together." The delegates could take some satisfaction in their accomplishments. They had created at least a semblance of an army and issued $3 million worth of bills of credit to equip and supply it.

The delegates left George Washington outside of Boston, grappling with "discord and confusion" in the ranks. But this only reflected in the military order the lack of unanimity among the politicians. It was hardly surprising when we consider the totally separate lives these men had lived, within their individual colonies, before they met to tackle the tremendous task of simultaneously forming a nation and fighting a war. Jefferson himself, for all his sophistication and scholarship, was a perfect example of provincial insularity. He wrote his brother-in-law about the death at Bunker Hill of the brilliant, young Massachusetts doctor-politician, Joseph Warren, describing him as "a man who seems to have been immensely valued in the North." The growth of a nation was a slow process, and among the many lessons Jefferson learned at Philadelphia, perhaps the most important was patience.

Although Jefferson refused to retreat an inch

from the principles he had already enunciated in his state papers, he still thought of his nation as the proud and triumphant British Empire into which he had been born. He showed this, as well as his gift for friendship, in response to a letter he received from John Randolph, not long after he returned to Virginia. Attorney General Randolph had decided that his loyalty to the king ran too deep to tolerate the revolutionary regime that had seized control of Virginia. Randolph was going "home," as Virginians of his era called England, and he wrote to his young friend Jefferson, offering to sell him the violin about which they had written a lighthearted contract some years before.

The violin was a Cremona, made by Nicola Amati in 1660. The body bore the Amati trademark of brilliant amber varnish; the fingerboard and tailpiece were ebony, the string pegs, ivory. Jefferson and the attorney general had agreed in ponderous legal terms that when the older man died, Jefferson would get the violin. But if capricious fate decreed the reverse, Randolph was entitled to select from the late Jefferson's library books to the value of £100.

Jefferson promptly accepted Randolph's new offer and added a personal note to the business paragraph, which revealed his inner thoughts on the crisis in the late summer of 1775. "I hope the returning wisdom of Great Britain will ere long put an end to this unnatural contest. There may be people to whose tempers and dispositions contention may be pleasing and who may therefore wish a continuance of confusion. But to me it is of all states, but one, the most horrid."

To this, Jefferson added a statement that announced for the first (but not the last) time the deep reluctance with which he left his family for the brawling world of war and politics. "My first wish is a restoration of our just rights; my second, a return of the happy period when consistently with duty I may withdraw myself totally from the public stage and pass the rest of my days in domestic ease and tranquillity, banishing every desire of afterwards even hearing what passes in the world."

Behind these yearning words lay the harsh knowledge that he would soon he leaving Monticello again to perform once more on this public stage. Earlier in the month of August the Virginia convention had voted Jefferson third place in the seven-man Continental delegation, a flattering testimony to his growing esteem in the eyes of the men who knew him best.

Congress met on September 5. But Jefferson did not arrive until September 25. Little Jane Randolph Jefferson, eighteen months old, died in her weeping mother's arms, another victim of the child-raising hazards of a century that did not yet understand what germs even were, much less how they did their deadly work.

Jefferson left his grieving, disconsolate wife with Francis and Elizabeth Eppes. Losing children was common at the time, but in Martha Jefferson's emotional nature the impact of grief ran far deeper than in most women. She apparently sank into a depression - or a combination of a physical illness and depression - that left her too weak or listless to write her husband a letter.

In Philadelphia, ensconced at Ben Randolph's house once more, Jefferson had set aside one day a week to write letters home. A month of wearying debate and committee work crept by, and he had not gotten a single answer. Finally, on November 7, he wrote to Francis Eppes in a tone that was nothing less than frantic: "I have never received a scrip of a pen from any mortal in Virginia since I left it, nor been able by any inquiries I could make to hear of my family . . . The suspense under which I am is too terrible to be endured. If any thing has happened, for God's sake let me know it." Eppes quickly reassured Jefferson that Martha was not seriously ill. But Jefferson wanted to hear the words from her own hand.

Meanwhile, Lord Dunmore, the royal governor, gave Jefferson something else to worry about - the menace of civil and racial war in Virginia. Dunmore established a base at Norfolk and began recruiting a loyalist army. Early in November, he took an even more ominous step, declaring he would give every black who joined his banner immediate freedom. A slave uprising was always a lurking dread in the back of every Virginian's mind, and this gesture made the awful reality more than a figment. Jefferson wrote another anxious letter to Martha, recommending that she retreat to their plantation at Poplar Forest in Bedford County, deep in the interior of the state, where Dunmore was unlikely to penetrate. To this, too, he received nothing but silence.

Congress, meanwhile, did little but watch the steady drift on both sides to all-out war. On November 9, they learned that George III had refused to receive Dickinson's olive-branch petition and on the August 23, 1775, had proclaimed the colonies to be in open rebellion. Parliament received the petition on November 7 and voted it down, eighty-three to thirty-three. But it was the king's contemptuous rejection that most affected Americans like Thomas Jefferson. On November 29, Jefferson wrote another letter to his friend John Randolph. The ostensible reason was to report to him the melancholy news of the death of his brother, Peyton Randolph, who succumbed to a stroke on November 22. Jefferson quickly expanded the letter into a discussion of the crisis.

Although Jefferson had spoken boldly and firmly to the king in the declarations and addresses he had already written, he had, like most Americans, still retained the hopeful opinion that the quarrel was between America and the greedy politicians in Parliament, and not with George III himself. The king's words and conduct had steadily eroded this fragile optimism, and now Jefferson wrote: "It is an immense misfortune to the whole empire to have a King of such a disposition at such a time. We are told and everything proves it true, that he is the bitterest enemy we have . . . To undo his empire there is but one truth more to learn, that after colonies have drawn the sword there is but one step more they can take. That step is now pressed upon us by the measures adopted as if they were afraid we would not take it."

Jefferson meant independence. "Believe me, dear sir," he wrote, "there is not in the British Empire a man who more cordially loves a union with Gr. Britain than I do. But by the God that made me, I will cease to exist before I yield to a connection on such terms as the British Parliament propose and in this I think I speak the sentiments of America."

In the last week in December, Jefferson abruptly abandoned Congress and Philadelphia and headed back to Virginia. There were political reasons for the move. Delegates came and went frequently; each colony only had a single vote, so no one felt any need to maintain the delegations at full strength at all times. Also, Jefferson had been appointed a member of the Committee of Safety for the colony of Virginia, as well as commander of the militia for his home county of Albemarle. With Lord Dunmore making more and more threatening noises, he may well have felt he was needed at home. But the paramount motive was his continuing anxiety about Martha.

For the next four months, he remained at Monticello, pushing ahead with the building of the mansion, taking on his own shoulders more and more of the housekeeping details. His wife was not Jefferson's only worry during these private months. On March 31, he recorded in his account books the loss of his mother, who died suddenly at the age of fifty-seven. We know little about Jane Randolph except that she was born in London in the parish of Shadwell and brought that musical name with her to christen the plantation on which she gave birth to six daughters and four sons. Only a family tradition tells us that she was a cheerful, outgoing person who, for a woman of her time, was unusually fond of writing and who composed lively, highly readable letters.

Shortly after her death, Jefferson experienced a blinding, debilitating pain that coursed from his temples through his entire head and throbbed relentlessly day and night for the next five weeks. It was his first recorded attack of what he called "the head ach." It was most likely a migraine, and it is the best possible proof that Jefferson was under a terrible personal strain during these months at Monticello. His mother's death may have contributed to this mental burden. But she was fifty-seven, considered old age in the eighteenth century, and all her children were grown. Almost certainly, the migraine points to a more profound and continuing worry - Martha. Jefferson had planned to leave for Philadelphia at the end of March; one might almost think that the attack was brought on by an unconscious desire to find some excuse, no matter how torturous, to delay his departure.

A fellow delegate, Thomas Nelson Jr., had brought his wife to Philadelphia with him, and he wrote to Jefferson, urging him to bring Martha along too. But eighteenth-century cities were unhealthy places and in spite of Nelson's assurance that his wife would "take all possible care of her" (which also hints that Martha's delicate health was common knowledge), Jefferson rejected the idea.

Early in May, he reluctantly left Monticello and, accompanied only by Jupiter, began the seven-day journey to the metropolis. He arrived on May 13 to find both the political and military aspects of the crisis on the brink of climax. The war news was both good and bad. Washington had driven the British out of Boston, and they had retreated to Halifax. But the understaffed, undersupplied American army that had fought a winter campaign to bring Canada into the union had been all but destroyed by disease and a stubborn British defense. They were now in alarming retreat before a revived and reinforced British Army of the North.

On the political front, a new author had exploded into print with "Common Sense," a pamphlet that had changed many minds about independence. Jefferson had read it long before he had arrived in Philadelphia. A fellow delegate had sent him a copy early in February. The author was Tom Paine, a rough, blunt, English-born freethinker who wasted no words. He called George III "a brute" and boldly summoned America to a rendezvous with history as a nation in her own right. The obvious determination of the king and his ministers to suppress American resistance with force made Paine's advice doubly persuasive.

In Philadelphia, Jefferson found a letter from his best friend, John Page, written a month before. "For God's sake declare the colonies independent at once and save us from ruin." This was but a single rivulet in what an exultant John Adams called "the torrent" for independence that rolled in upon the Congress every day.

But those who hoped, however dimly, for some kind of reconciliation as an alternative to all-out war, still had strong voices in Congress. Only three short months before, an important committee had declared that independence was most emphatically not America's goal. Everyone in Philadelphia knew that the real decision would be made, not in the Pennsylvania State House, but in Williamsburg where the Virginia convention was meeting on May 15. Though Massachusetts may have struck the spark that sent the Revolution flaming, the New England personality was too abrasive to bring the colonies together under her leadership. Virginia had taken the lead in almost every significant step since George III had closed the port of Boston.

All Jefferson could do was wait patiently for instructions from "his country," as he still called Virginia. What was uppermost in his mind is evident in his May 16 letter to Thomas Nelson Jr. "I am here in the same uneasy, anxious state in which I was the last fall without Mrs. Jefferson who could not come with me." As for independence, his opinion on the subject certainly did not equal the vehemence of Richard Henry Lee, who was writing Patrick Henry: "Ages yet unborn and millions existing at present must rue or bless that assembly [of Virginia] on which their happiness or misery will so eminently depend." Jefferson merely noted that in the upper counties, such as Albemarle, he had taken "great pains to inquire into the sentiment of the people" and found "nine out of ten are for it."

If Virginia voted for independence, Jefferson hoped "respect will be expressed to the right of opinion in other colonies who may happen to differ from them." He was, in fact, much more concerned about the possibility that the Virginia convention, once it voted to break the bond with England, would immediately take up the problems of forming a new government, and this made him wish he was not 300 miles away in Philadelphia. "It is," he said, "a work of the most interesting nature and such as every individual would wish to have his voice in." He even suggested to Nelson that it might be a good idea to recall the Virginia delegation, except for "one or two to give information to Congress" and let them join in the work of government building, that was, he said, "the whole object of the present controversy; for should a bad government be instituted for us in the future it had been as well to accept at first the bad one offered to us from beyond the water without the risk and expence of contest."

Jefferson rushed to Edmund Pendleton, speaker of the Virginia legislature, a draft of the sort of constitution he thought Virginia should have. It was a remarkable document, especially when we consider that it was written in great haste. It called for wider democracy - anyone with twenty-five acres of farmland or a quarter of an acre of town land could vote - and it explicitly guaranteed religious freedom, freedom of the press, and abolished the antiquated inheritance laws that Virginia had brought from England. It was much too radical for the conservative majority in the Virginia Assembly. All they adopted from Jefferson's draft was his preamble that was a burning recital of the wrongs England had committed against Virginia, thus justifying the formation of a new and independent government.

Not long after Jefferson fired off this revolutionary constitution, his anxiety over Martha became overwhelming, and he wrote two letters that came close to canceling his rendezvous with world history. The first was to his friend Dr. George Gilmer, who was representing Albemarle in the Virginia convention, and the second was to Edmund Pendleton, the chairman of the convention. The letters are lost, but we know from references to them that Jefferson asked the assembly not to re-elect him to the Continental Congress and requested permission to go home as soon as possible. Gilmer was unable to attend on the day the convention elected delegates for Philadelphia, and he passed the chore of getting Jefferson excused on to another friend, Edmund Randolph, who "urged it in decent terms." All he got for his effort was a "swarm of wasps about my ears who seemed suspicious that I designed to prejudice you." Jefferson's letter to Chairman Pendleton had not arrived and after a half hour's debate, the assembly rejected Jefferson's plea and elected him and four other delegates for another year's service in Philadelphia. Thus, with an irony that often seems to be history's favorite sport, Jefferson remained at his post, bemoaning his fate and fretting over every post rider who arrived from Virginia without a letter from Martha.

On June 7, 1776, in the humid State House, where Jefferson sat with his fellow congressmen each day, Richard Henry Lee, in obedience to instructions from Virginia, laid before the house a historic resolution.

> That these united colonies are and of right ought to be, free and independent states, that they are absolved from all allegiance to the British crown, and that all political connections between them and the State of Great Britain is, and ought to be, totally dissolved.
>
> That it is expedient forthwith to take the most effectual measures for forming foreign alliances.
>
> That a plan of confederation be prepared and transmitted to the respective colonies for their consideration and approbation.

John Adams leaped to his feet and seconded the motion. If he and Lee had any hopes that they could force the issue to an immediate vote, they were soon dashed. The moderates made a motion to postpone debate for a day. On June 8, Saturday, Lee, Adams, and George Wythe debated ferociously with James Wilson and John Dickinson of Pennsylvania, Robert R. Livingston of New York, and Edward Rutledge of South Carolina. Jefferson did not say a single word all day, or on the following Monday when the war of words was renewed with rising ferocity. But he was keenly aware of the momentous nature of the occasion, and he sat in his seat, taking more voluminous notes than anyone else, even Charles Thomson, the secretary of Congress.

Basically, the moderates argued against the timing of the declaration. They pointed out that the people of the middle colonies (Maryland, Delaware, Pennsylvania, New Jersey, and New York) were undecided about independence. It would be better to wait for them to ripen, lest they secede and weaken the union. Adams, Lee, and their supporters argued that the declaration was merely the statement of an already existing fact. They asserted that "the people wait for us to lead the way," and argued that a majority, even in the middle colonies, were for the measure even though their local representatives hesitated to approve it. Above all, they argued that it "would be vain to wait either weeks or months for perfect unanimity since it was impossible that all men should ever become of one sentiment on any question."

On and on the orators rumbled until President John Hancock's gavel fell, adjourning the house once more with no agreement in sight. The next day, when the undaunted moderates rose to renew the battle, the independence men decided to admit temporary defeat. As Jefferson said later, it was clear that New York, New Jersey, Pennsylvania, Delaware, Maryland, and even South Carolina were "not yet matured for falling from the parent stem."

Both sides agreed to postpone further debate for three weeks. This would give the uncertain colonies time to write home to their local assemblies for instructions. Meanwhile, there was no reason why a committee should not be appointed to draw up a possible declaration of independence. Everyone agreed on the vital importance of such a document; it was not something that should be thrown together hurriedly in a few brief days. Nominations were accepted for a committee, and in a matter of minutes Secretary Charles Thomson was inscribing in the minutes: "The members chosen: Mr. Jefferson, Mr. J. Adams, Mr. Franklin, Mr. Sherman, and Mr. R. R. Livingston."

Ben Franklin was incapacitated by an attack of gout. Ten days after the committee was formed, he wrote to Washington that it had kept him "from Congress and company almost ever since you left us, so that I know little of what has pass'd there, except that a declaration of independence is preparing . . ."

Neither Sherman nor Livingston had any literary reputation, and the question of who was to draft the declaration descended to a choice between John Adams and Thomas Jefferson. Years later Adams recalled that Jefferson had offered the job to Adams, who promptly replied: "I will not."

"You should do it!" declared Jefferson.

"Oh, no!" was Adams's response.

"Why will you not? You ought to do it," said Jefferson.

"I will not," Adams repeated.

"Why?" asked Jefferson.

"Reasons enough," said Adams.

"What can be your reasons?" inquired Jefferson.

Adams responded: "Reason first - you are a Virginian, and a Virginian ought to appear at the head of this business. Reason second - I am obnoxious, suspected, and unpopular. You are very much otherwise. Reason third - you can write ten times better than I can."

"Well, if you are decided, I will do as well as I can," Jefferson conceded.

To which Adams agreed, "Very well. When you have drawn it up, we will have a meeting."

Jefferson went to work. He had recently moved from Ben Randolph's house to new quarters in a fine brick house, three stories high, on the southwest corner of Market and Seventh streets. It belonged to a bricklayer named Graff, and Jefferson had taken two rooms on the second floor - a bedroom and a parlor, separated by a stairs between them.

Before he left cabinetmaker Randolph, Jefferson purchased a piece of his handiwork made to his own specifications - a portable desk, which he later described as "plain, neat, convenient and taking no more room on the writing table than a moderate quarto volume, and yet displays itself sufficiently for any writing." In Graff's sunny second-floor parlor, he set up this self-designed "writing box" on a convenient table beside a supply of paper, ink, and pens.

Years later, Jefferson recalled that he consulted "neither book nor pamphlet." He had no desire to find out "new principles or new arguments never before thought of." His purpose was to "place before mankind the common sense of the subject in terms so plain and firm as to command their assent." He did not even aim at "originality of principle or sentiment," in the individual sense of these terms. The declaration "was intended to be an expression of the American mind and to give to that expression the proper tone and spirit called for by the occasion."

But there were other more personal emotions fermenting in Jefferson's mind. One was the lurking sense that he was risking - perhaps even sacrificing - his beloved Martha to this cause. "Every letter brings me such an account of her health, that it is with great pain I can stay here," he had recently written to John Page. Another more visible worry was the rumor that he was somehow being downgraded by the politicians of his home state because his distaste for violent political conflict had inclined him to be friendly to men on both sides of the widening conservative-radical gulf.

To his friend Will Fleming, who had been disabled by a musket shot to his chest in Dunsmore's War (1774), Jefferson wrote: "It is a painful situation to be 300 miles from one's country and thereby open to secret assassination without a possibility of self-defense. I am willing to hope nothing of this kind has been done in my case, and yet I cannot be easy. If any doubt has arisen as to me, my country will have my political creed in the form of a declaration &c., which I was lately directed to draw." It is clear that along with an intention to express the "American mind," Jefferson poured deep personal anguish and burning personal conviction into the declaration.

Even if we did not know these things, the emotion is visible in the dramatic cadences of the declaration itself. All we have to do is compare it to the style of Jefferson's preamble to the Virginia constitution. This began with a legal "whereas" and then listed grievances singly, beginning each one with a clumsy participle. Two examples are enough.

By putting his negative on laws the most wholesome & necessary for the public good.

By denying his governors permission to pass

laws of the most immediate and pressing importance.

This was Jefferson, the lawyer, speaking. When he bent his head over Ben Randolph's writing box on those hot mornings in mid-June in Philadelphia, he was no lawyer drawing a brief for an interested client, he was an anguished, deeply involved human being who felt the momentous nature of the document he was writing, both for his personal and public self. The rhythms of the opening paragraph throb with a deeper, richer timbre than anything Jefferson ever wrote.

When in the course of human events it becomes necessary for one people to dissolve the political bands which have connected them with another, and to assume among the powers of the earth a separate and equal station to which the laws of nature and of nature's God entitle them, a decent respect to the opinions of mankind requires that they should declare the causes which impel them to this separation.

However, Jefferson did not let his emotion interfere with literary craftsmanship. He worked diligently on the declaration in the first days of composition, often making changes in the wording. A fragment of one of his early drafts, which Jefferson had ripped up and used to take notes on another matter, was not found among the mass of his papers until 1943. On this, the earliest existing (though incomplete) draft of the declaration, no less than forty-three of the 156 words were additions or substitutions for words and phrases that had been deleted. In the text that was for almost two centuries considered "the rough draft" all these changes appear intact. Thus, it is now known that the rough draft was close to a final copy. But even then Jefferson continued to polish it.

The final changes he made on this so-called rough draft are by no means insignificant. The opening lines first read: "When in the course of human events it becomes necessary for a people to advance from that subordination in which they have hitherto remained." The sentence ended with "change" instead of "separation."

In the next paragraph, he first wrote: "We hold these truths to be sacred & undeniable that all men are created equal & independent, that from that equal creation they derive rights inherent and inalienable, among which are the preservation of life and liberty and the pursuit of happiness."

How much better is the final effort. "We hold these truths to be self-evident: that all men are created equal; that they are endowed by their creator with certain inalienable rights."

What were these rights? In a line that he never had to change, Jefferson summed them up in words that are forever linked with his name - "Life, liberty and the pursuit of happiness." The idea, of course, was not original with him. As early as 1770, Pennsylvanian James Wilson, in a pamphlet on the legislative authority of the British Parliament, had written: "The consequence is that the happiness of the society is the first law of every government." Jefferson's fellow Virginian, George Mason, had drafted a bill of rights that was adopted by the Virginia Assembly. In it, Mason had written that men had certain inherent rights - "the enjoyment of life and liberty, with the means of acquiring and possessing property, and pursuing and obtaining happiness and safety." How much more concise, and at the same time more majestic, is Jefferson's phrase.

Almost as famous are the words Jefferson wrote next. "That to secure these rights governments are instituted among men, deriving their just powers from the consent of the governed." Again the idea can be traced to a dozen writers, including the English philosopher John Locke, James Wilson, and George Mason. But Wilson wrote: "All lawful government is founded on the consent of those who are subject to it." Mason wrote: "All power is vested in and consequently derived from the people." Again Jefferson created a more compact and memorable statement of the basic idea. He was earning a rich dividend on his youthful struggles with "Old Coke," who taught him, he once said, "never to use two words where one would do." (Old Coke referred to Sir Edward Coke, an influential jurist in Renaissance England who fought for the supremacy of Common Law over the monarchy.)

In the third clause of his bill of rights, Mason had written:

> Government is or ought to be instituted for the common benefit, protection, and security of the people, nation, or community; of all the various modes and forms of government that is best which is capable of producing the greatest degree of happiness and safety, and is most effectually secured against the danger of mal-administration; and that when any government shall be found inadequate or contrary to these purposes, a majority of the community has the indubitable, unalienable right to reform, alter, or abolish it, in such manner as shall be judged most conducive to the public weal.

Here is what Jefferson does to this pedestrian statement of a great ideal:

> Whenever any form of government becomes destructive of these ends, it is the right of the people to alter or to abolish it, & to institute new government, laying its foundation on such principles and organizing its powers in such form, as to them shall seem most likely to effect their safety and happiness.

This magnificent statement of the rights of man has been the heart of the declaration's immortality. But to Jefferson and his audience, by far the most important part of the document was the indictment of George III for creating the crisis. Instead of beginning the list of the king's crimes with a weak participle, he used again and again the words "He has."

> He has refused his assent to laws the most wholesome and necessary for the public good;

> He has forbidden his governors to pass laws of immediate and pressing importance . . .

> He has dissolved representative houses repeatedly and continually, for opposing with manly firmness his invasions of the rights of the people . . .

> He has made our judges dependent on his will alone . . .

No less than nineteen times Jefferson repeated this "He has" until it became a mournful but meaningful bell tolling the death of American affection for George III.

As a climax - and for Jefferson the most significant item in this grim bill of particulars - Jefferson wrote a paragraph that tells us more about himself, personally, than anything else in the declaration.

He has waged cruel war against human nature itself, violating its most sacred rights of life and liberty in the persons of a distant people who never offended him, captivating and carrying them into slavery in another hemisphere, or to incur miserable death in their transportation thither. This piratical warfare, the opprobrium of infidel powers, is the warfare of the Christian King of Great Britain. Determined to keep open a market where Men should be bought and sold, he has prostituted his negative for suppressing every legislative attempt to prohibit or to restrain this execrable commerce and that this assemblage of horrors might want no fact of distinguished dye, he is now exciting those very people to rise in arms among us, and to purchase that liberty of which he has deprived them, by murdering the people upon whom he also obtruded them; thus paying off former crimes committed against the liberties of one people, with crimes which he urges them to commit against the lives of another.

Thus Jefferson declared to the world his passionate loathing of slavery. Among his earliest legal cases - one for which he waived a fee - he had pleaded for the liberty of a mulatto grandson of a white woman and a black slave by boldly arguing that slavery was a violation of a man's natural right to freedom. One of the reasons he so desperately wanted to join his fellow Virginians in their constitutional convention was his wish to lead a fight for the gradual abolition of slavery in his "country." His draft constitution, which the convention ignored, had contained an explicit provision for such a measure.

Now Jefferson turned to another question that loomed large in the minds of his fellow Americans - their relation with the British people, as distinguished from the British Parliament. Jefferson showed his boldness by writing a fierce indictment of them as well. Then, in a sonorous closing paragraph, Jefferson declared "these colonies to be free and independent states." Finally, third in the roll call of his immortal phrases, came the sentence: "And for the support of this declaration we mutually pledge to each other our lives, our fortunes, and our sacred honor."

Jefferson showed a rough draft of the declaration to John Adams, Roger Sherman, and Robert Livingston. They suggested a few word changes and one or two minor additions. This is evident from a recently discovered letter from Jefferson to Benjamin Franklin, probably written Friday morning, June 21. "The enclosed paper has been read and with some small alterations approved of by the committee," Jefferson wrote. "Will Doctr. Franklyn be so good as to peruse it and suggest such alterations as his more enlarged view of the subject will dictate?"

Franklin had only a few word changes to suggest. Some scholars feel it was he, not Jefferson, who changed "sacred and undeniable" to self-evident. Jefferson made what he called "a fair copy" of the declaration and with the approval of the full committee, submitted it to Congress on June 28, 1776. Congress ordered it to "lie on the table," undiscussed and unvoted upon, for the next two days. We can be sure, however, that it was not unread. John Adams had already made a copy, and Jefferson had made several. Almost certainly there were others. But for a moment, the document was in limbo. Congress had yet to make the crucial decision that would bring it to life or consign it to oblivion. July 1 was the fateful day on which Congress was to reconsider Richard Henry Lee's resolution for independence.

The day dawned hot and clear and from their lodgings around Philadelphia, the delegates walked to the State House in a saturnine mood. Independence and anti-independence men formed on opposite sides of the room; the conservatives' leader, John Dickinson, was lean and pale in a plum-colored coat and breeches. On the independence side, the ranks were thin. Richard Henry Lee and George Wythe were still in Virginia. New representatives from New Jersey, who John Adams had predicted would "vote plump" for independence, had not yet arrived. Nor had new instructions for the Maryland delegates, which Samuel Chase had vowed to send from Annapolis. Delaware, with two delegates present, was temporarily a cipher, because one was for, the other against independence. None of these states had deserted the cause. Their leaders had gone home to fight for it, but distances were great, travel slow and local assemblies were as divided about independence as the Congress.

At noon, John Hancock stepped down from the president's chair, thereby signaling that Congress was resolving itself into a committee of the whole, in which debate and vote would be unofficial. Benjamin Harrison, his hearty good nature cloaked in official seriousness, took his seat as chairman for the committee of the whole, and the debate began.

John Dickinson spoke first. A grimly earnest, deeply sincere man, he proclaimed his indifference to personal popularity. It was the survival of the nation that was at stake, he insisted. To abandon the protection of Great Britain by declaring independence now, Dickinson vowed, "would be like destroying our house in winter and exposing a growing family before we have got another shelter." As he spoke, the doorman gave John Adams an envelope postmarked Annapolis. Adams tore it open and read: "I am this moment from the House with an unan: vote of our convention for independence . . . Your friend, S. Chase."

John Adams rose to answer Dickinson. Out of a passion as deep and personal as Jefferson himself felt for the cause, Adams gave the greatest speech of his career. In later years Jefferson said it had "a power of thought and expression that moved us from our seats." Nature, meanwhile, added to the drama. The smiling summer sky above the State House had slowly changed to an ominous black. Thunder rumbled and crashed, shaking the windows; lightning streaked the gloom. Candles were lit, and Adams spoke on, out-roaring the storm. He was still on his feet when into the chamber stalked three rain-soaked delegates from New Jersey with instructions to declare for independence.

Harrison called for a vote. The four New England states, Virginia, North Carolina, and Georgia were for separation. But New York had specific instructions against voting for independence, although their delegates lamely explained that personally they favored it. Delaware was divided, and Pennsylvania and South Carolina voted nay. The worst fears of many Congressmen seemed on the brink of coming true. Four states, almost a third of the thirteen colonies, were against independence. Instead of unifying the colonies, the Declaration threatened to become the issue that divided and destroyed them.

Quickly, Edward Rutledge of South Carolina rose

and suggested postponing an official vote until the following day. The idea was gratefully accepted, and Harrison's gavel fell, dissolving the committee of the whole.

A night of frantic negotiation and desperate action began. An express rider was rushed to Dover, Delaware, to summon lawyer Caesar Rodney, to rescue his state with his pro-independence vote. Rutledge was lectured on the dangers of disunity. John Dickinson was bluntly told that his attitude was not shared by the majority of his fellow Pennsylvanians, and the recent elections to the Pennsylvania assembly, where pro-independence men had won handily, were offered as proof.

The next morning, Tuesday, July 2, President Hancock took his seat and called for an official vote "in full congress assembled." Caesar Rodney, splattered with mud and water, was in his seat from Delaware, after an eighty-mile all-night ride through pelting rain. Edward Rutledge, "for the sake of unanimity," had changed South Carolina's mind. John Dickinson and his friend Robert Morris stayed home, giving Pennsylvania a three-to-two majority in favor of independence. So the momentous vote was recorded, twelve states for independence and New York abstaining only because new instructions had not yet arrived from her assembly. (They would take another thirteen days to reach Philadelphia.) The torrent for independence had become a flood. To his wife Abigail, John Adams wrote: "The 2nd day of July, 1776, will be the most memorable epocha in the history of America. I am apt to believe that it will be celebrated by succeeding generations as the great anniversary festival."

That was a wholly sincere, perfectly logical prophecy from a man immersed in the moment-to-moment drama of independence. But John Adams's great speech vanished without a man recording a single word of it. Thomas Jefferson's declaration, which Congress now undertook to consider in detail, was to be published and republished around the world. That was why July 4, when the declaration was approved, and not July 2, when independence was voted, became America's Independence Day. It is a testimony to the enormous power of the written word.

The next two days were not happy ones for Jefferson. No author likes to see his work edited, and Jefferson now had to sit and endure the criticism of not one but a squadron of editors. The declaration was scrutinized, word by word, line by line, paragraph by paragraph, with Congress sitting once more as a committee of the whole. Before Jefferson's shocked eyes and ears, whole paragraphs were ripped out of the document he had labored so hard to perfect. His comments, made years later, still reflect the pain of the author who is seeing his efforts mauled by men whose purposes were decidedly unliterary.

"The pusillanimous idea that we had friends in England worth keeping terms with still haunted the minds of many. For this reason, those passages which conveyed censures on the people of England were struck out, lest they should give them offense."

Next, from north as well as south, came objections to the paragraph Jefferson felt was among the most important in the document - the slashing attack on the slave trade. Gentlemen from South Carolina and Georgia proclaimed themselves angrily in favor of continuing to import slaves. "Our northern brethren," Jefferson wrote, "also I believe felt a little tender over those censures; for though their people had very few slaves themselves, yet they had been pretty considerable carriers of them to others."

None of these changes were accomplished without vigorous debate, and John Adams was in the forefront with his usual blunt ferocity, "fighting fearlessly for every word," Jefferson testified later. If Jefferson had already "touched" Adams's heart with his forthrightness, now it was the stumpy New Englander's turn to forge on his side a debt of friendship that Jefferson never forgot. But unity was the vital necessity in 1776, and Adams and his supporters got nowhere with their protests. Let South Carolina and Georgia have their slave trade, the majority decided. After the war was won, if a nation was formed, then would be time enough to do something about slavery. If, on the other hand, the colonies decided to pursue independent courses (at this point no one was entirely certain), then slavery was their own dirty business. So Jefferson could only sit in obvious misery and watch Benjamin Harrison, once more presiding over the committee as a whole, draw his official pen through the fiery phrases.

Sympathetic though any writer must be with Jefferson's anguish over these "mutilations," an objective reading of the declaration makes it clear that, on the whole, Congress improved the finished product. They added one of the more resounding final phrases, "with a firm reliance on the protection of Divine Providence." Even their surgery, for motives wholly political, had a healthy literary effect. The final result was a leaner, harder-hitting document.

In spite of the editing, the declaration was still Jefferson's creation. As one historian summed it up, "His pen had written it, his spirit brooded over it, giving light to the whole..." But Jefferson did not feel that way on July 4, 1776, when the final version was read aloud to a satisfied Congress. John Hancock took the president's chair once more, and Congress voted its official approval. Whether the members present signed it then, or later in the month, is a subject that historians have been debating for almost 100 years. According to Jefferson, a copy was signed on July 4. An "engrossed" or parchment copy was signed on July 19.

Benjamin Franklin and other friends tried to console Jefferson, but Jefferson's pain over the amputation of so many of his favorite phrases and clauses remained acute. When he sent copies of the final declaration to his friends in Virginia, he made a point of enclosing a copy of his original draft as well. A few, such as Edmund Pendleton, were gentlemanly enough to assure him that Congress had "altered it much for the worse." Richard Henry Lee flattered him unctuously, assuring him that though the manuscript had been "mangled," it was nevertheless "wonderful . . . the thing is in its nature so good that no cookery can spoil the dish for the palates of free men." Only his old friend John Page had the good sense to ignore the implied comparison and simply tell Jefferson, "I am highly pleased with your declaration."

Meanwhile, Jefferson's thoughts were already returning to Monticello. On July 4, he bought no less than seven pairs of gloves and a number of other items of feminine finery for Martha. Throughout the month of July, while Congress held melancholy hearings on the disastrous retreat of the American army that had hoped to conquer Canada, and debated Articles of Confederation, Jefferson's anxiety about Martha's health continued to mount. On July 15, he wrote to Francis Eppes:

"I wish I could be better satisfied on the point of Patty's recovery. I had not heard from her at all for two posts before, and no letter from herself now." On July 23, he was again writing to Eppes. "I have received no letter this week, which lays me under great anxiety."

Meanwhile, the declaration was circulating throughout the colonies and was being proclaimed, in accordance with the orders of President John Hancock, "in such a mode that the people may be universally informed of it." Philadelphia saw the first proclamation on July 8. Some forty congressmen, no doubt including Jefferson, watched while it was read from a scaffold in the State House yard to a huge crowd of people. "Three cheers rendered the welkin," John Adams said. "The battalions paraded on the Common . . . the bells rang all day and almost all night." On July 9, George Washington had it read before the army at New York and reported to Congress that "the measure seems to have their most hearty assent, the expressions and behavior of both officers and men testifying their warmest approbation of it." On the Battery, civilian New Yorkers pulled down the leaden statue of George III and melted it into bullets.

Providence, Rhode Island, celebrated the publication with thirteen volleys from the ships in the harbor. In Baltimore, patriots carted an effigy of George III through the town, and then it was "committed to the flames amidst the acclamations of many hundreds - the just reward of a tyrant." It soon became evident that the declaration had done more to unite the colonies than any other single pronouncement of Congress. As time passed, men also realized that Jefferson's magnificent phrasing was the vital factor in its electrifying impact on hesitant and divided minds.

But for the moment, Jefferson's authorship was known only to a small handful of his friends and fellow congressmen. In July 1776, everyone was keenly aware that the declaration was nothing less than an act of treason. Elias Dayton of New Jersey summed up the prevailing state of mind when he wrote, "As to my title, I know not whether it will be honorable or dishonorable: the issue of war must settle it. Perhaps our Congress will be exalted on a high gallows." For another eight months, Congress kept even the names of the signers a closely guarded secret. But knowledge of Jefferson's authorship slowly filtered down to the common man, who read those opening phrases about equality and the pursuit of happiness as a promise of a better future, and began to admire both the words and the man who wrote them.

4

For the moment, however, Jefferson remained an obscure, harassed delegate to a Congress that bickered through the sweltering heat of August over what he called "the minutia of the confederation." Jefferson's thoughts were in Virginia. Martha had sent him a letter, plaintively begging him to come home. Impulsively, Jefferson had promised her he would be at her side by the middle of August.

Then, to his mounting distress, the older members of the Virginia delegation found various excuses to absent themselves until only he and Carter Braxton were left. Next, Braxton also anticipated Jefferson's desire, by announcing on July 20 that he was going home within two days. This left Jefferson the only guardian of Virginia's vote in Congress, and thus made it impossible for him to leave. He had already written to Richard Henry Lee, begging him to return to Philadelphia to relieve him. On July 21, Lee had written casually that he would be on his way on September 3. This answer drew from Jefferson a cry of anguish. "For God's sake, for your country's sake and for my sake, come," he begged. "I receive by every post such accounts of the state of Mrs. Jefferson's health that it will be impossible for me to disappoint her expectation of seeing me at the time I have promised." At the end of the letter, after a few more hurried sentences about Congressional business, he added one more plea. "I pray you to come. I am under a sacred obligation to go home."

But Lee could not be hurried, and Jefferson had to spend the rest of the broiling month of August in Philadelphia, where he dutifully served on several committees, none of which involved matters that could justify his absence from home when he was so badly needed. Jefferson recommended a seal for the United States of America (his motto, "*e pluribus unum*," was later adopted but not his artwork), debated with Pennsylvanians and others the conflicting claims the various states had to western lands, and wrote a long report on gold and silver coins full of tables which are models of scientific exactitude. Though he did not realize it, the report was a major step toward one of his least recognized achievements, the creation of the American monetary system. He also corresponded with Edmund Pendleton about revising the laws of Virginia. But his mind and heart were at The Forest where Patty was staying with Francis Eppes and his wife.

Jefferson had rushed a letter to her, forbidding her to journey to Monticello and become involved in the plantation's responsibilities without him. In another letter, his anxiety had impelled him to write Edmund Pendleton that he hoped he could retire completely from politics. The alarmed elder statesman, who had just finished telling Jefferson how badly he was needed to help create a new government for Virginia, urged him in reply to "get cured of your wish to retire so early in life from the memory of man, and exercise your talents for the nurture of our new constitution."

Finally, on September 1, Jefferson could stand it no longer and even though Lee had not yet arrived, he settled his various accounts, bought some hats and guitar strings and on September 3, 1776, set out for Monticello. He picked up Martha en route and for a few all too brief weeks they enjoyed the autumn beauty of their mountain.

In later years, a visitor to Monticello left a vivid description of this season of the year at Monticello. It was a paean of praise to the way "the imperial mantle of forest, wrought into brilliant dyes by the frost and sunshine, seemed in the soft haze to float down the graceful slope." But the beauties of nature, the joy with which Jefferson's young daughter "Patsy" and Martha greeted him could not disguise the fact that his wife was seriously ill. Some physicians who have studied the scanty evidence believe that Martha Jefferson was suffering from diabetes. Others think that she was simply a fragile, emotionally dependent person who became depressed when she was separated from her husband and this, in turn, had a disastrous effect on her physical health.

Certainly Jefferson seemed to feel that his presence was literally vital to her well-being. On October 20, he took her to a doctor for an examination, and she was pronounced well enough to go with him to Williamsburg where the Virginia convention was meeting. His old mentor, George Wythe, was in Philadelphia serving out his term as a delegate, and the Jeffersons persuaded him with no difficulty to lend them his handsome brick house on the west side of the Palace green in Williamsburg. "Make use of the house and furniture. I shall be happy if anything of mine can contribute to make your and Mrs. Jefferson's residence in Williamsburg comfortable," wrote this kindly man.

The house and grounds were a plantation in miniature. Vegetables in abundance were available from the garden and Jefferson undoubtedly made sure that Martha's diet was as healthy as the knowledge of the day could make it. He himself was passionately fond of vegetables and fruit and so little interested in meat he was almost a vegetarian. Behind the house was a pleasure garden, where Martha and her husband, with their enthusiasm for growing things, spent many an hour strolling the brick and marl paths lined with tree-box topiary.

The Jeffersons were just beginning to enjoy the Wythe house when a letter from Philadelphia came swirling in by special express, throwing both husband and wife into new turmoil. Congress had nominated Jefferson as one of three commissioners to go to France and negotiate a treaty of alliance. It was a striking testimony to how deeply Jefferson had impressed his fellow congressmen. The other commissioners were Benjamin Franklin and Silas Deane, who was already in France and had established important contacts with the French court.

Moreover, the words of President John Hancock's letter made it clear that Congress was very much aware of the honor and the importance of the mission. "It is with particular pleasure I congratulate you on the occasion," Hancock wrote. In an accompanying letter, Richard Henry Lee was even more explicit, describing the treaty as "this all-important business." He added that "the great abilities and unshaken virtue necessary for the execution of what the safety of America does so capitally rest upon, has directed the Congress in their choice . . . In my judgment the most eminent services that the greatest of her sons can do America will not more essentially serve her and honor themselves than a successful negotiation with France."

Here, thrust upon Jefferson as a gift - more than a gift, a high honor - was the opportunity to fulfill that youthful dream of seeing the Old World - seeing it moreover as a man of importance, not a mere student counting his pennies and scratching for introductions to minor dignitaries. Congress was even stretching its slender resources to the utmost to accommodate him. "If it is your pleasure, one of our armed vessels will meet you in any river in Virginia that you choose," wrote Richard Henry Lee.

For three days, Jefferson was a man in torment, trying to make a decision. Should he take Martha with him? A look at her wan face and the way she leaned invalid fashion on his strong arm when they strolled in Wythe's garden scotched that idea. Only someone in the best physical health could be expected to endure six to eight weeks on the Atlantic in late autumn, eating stale ship's food and being confined to a cramped, sunless cabin by heavy weather. Should he go alone? Martha Jefferson was not the sort of woman who would use her illness as a weapon in an argument. It was not necessary. The pain in her eyes at the mere proposal that she could bear a separation of perhaps a year, even two years, silenced Jefferson's tongue.

Finally, on the third day, Jefferson sat down in George Wythe's book-lined study and wrote one of the most mournful letters of his life. "No cares of my own person, nor yet for my private affairs would have induced one moment's hesitation to accept the charge," he said. "But circumstances very peculiar in the situation of my family, such as neither permit me to leave nor to carry it, compel me to ask leave to decline a service so honorable and at the same time so important to the American cause. The necessity under which I labor, and the conflict I have undergone for three days, during which I could not determine to dismiss your messenger, will I hope plead my pardon with Congress . . ."

Jefferson was too embarrassed even to reply to Richard Henry Lee. That acerbic gentleman declined to show the least understanding of Jefferson's agonizing position. From Philadelphia, Lee had written: "As I have received no answer to the letter I wrote you by the express from Congress, I conclude it has miscarried. I heard with much regret that you had declined both the voyage and your seat in Congress. No man feels more deeply than I do, the love of, and the loss of, private enjoyment; but let attention to these be universal, and we are gone beyond redemption, lost in the deep perdition of slavery."

Jefferson's dilemma was literally insoluble. He could not admit, even to himself, that his wife was seriously ill. Even if he could admit it, an instinctive reticence about his private life made him shrink from blurting out the news in starkly sentimental terms. Thus the private torment, the worry about Martha's health, became a public embarrassment, making Jefferson seem a hypocrite who wrote glowing phrases but was not willing to shoulder the burden of turning his lofty ideas into realities.

This sense of public censure drove Jefferson to throw all his energy into his work as a delegate to the Virginia Assembly. He was also deeply convinced that the state's laws had many "vicious points which urgently required reformation" as holdovers from Virginia's royal past. Still another reason for the importance he attached to this work was the position of Virginia, as the largest, most populous state in the new union. Where Virginia led, others would inevitably follow. So Jefferson felt that he was legislating both for his native state and for the American nation.

Within a few days after taking his seat as a delegate, Jefferson introduced a series of bills aimed at removing the aristocratic bias from Virginia society. The base of the aristocracy's power was two inheritance laws - entail and primogeniture. Thanks to entail, the head of a great estate, such as Landon Carter, could literally forbid his descendants to break it up, in order to settle family arguments or reward favorite sons and daughters. The goal was the preservation of the Carter name and influence, beyond the uncertainties of a particular generation's talents or intelligence. If Landon Carter III turned out to be an idiot, and Landon Carter IV a genius, the great estate would still be there, more or less intact for him to build upon. Primogeniture had a similar aristocratic purpose. If a man died without a will, his inheritance automatically went to the eldest son.

In this same crowded period, Jefferson collided with Virginia aristocrats over still another matter crucial to the future development of the American nation. For several decades, settlers had been drifting over the Blue Ridge Mountains into an area vaguely known as Kentucky. In this same uncharted west, the great landholders of Virginia had laid claims to huge tracts that they had purchased on credit or procured by influence with the crown. The pioneers and these speculative land companies were soon in a state of semi-warfare, with the settlers angrily refusing to surrender land that they had cleared and farmed at the risk of their lives, merely because some traveling representative of a land company flourished a piece of paper and asserted ownership.

The biggest of these companies, set up by one Richard Henderson of North Carolina with the backing of a number of prominent Virginians, actually attempted to create a state of Transylvania and sent a delegate to the Continental Congress in the hope of winning recognition. Jefferson wrecked this scheme by sponsoring a bill dividing the area into three counties and giving the western, anti-aristocratic portion of Virginia six new representatives. The bill also specified that no one could be made a civil or military officer in these new counties if he had taken an oath of office "to the pretended government of Richard Henderson, Gent. & Company."

These bills won Jefferson the enmity of some of the most powerful men in Virginia. In an explosive letter to George Washington about the bill abolishing entails, Landon Carter compared Jefferson to "a midday drunkard." (He also gave grudging credit to Jefferson's growing reputation by sneering at "the famous T. J-n!") But to Jefferson it was all part of a fight to "make an opening for the aristocracy of virtue and talent . . . essential to a well-ordered republic." It was in his view the gentlest and most civilized of revolutions. "No violence was necessary, no deprivation of natural right, but rather an enlargement of it . . ."

Against him, as the chief spokesman of the "ancient establishments," was Edmund Pendleton, whom Jefferson called "the ablest man in debate I have ever met with . . . cool, smooth and persuasive." A veteran parliamentarian, Pendleton was as tenacious as he was skillful. "If he lost the main battle, he returned upon you," Jefferson said, "and regained so much of it as to make it a drawn one by dexterous maneuvers, skirmishes in detail and the recovery of small advantages which, little singly, were important all together. You never knew when you were clear of him . . ." But again, in his recollections of the often feverish debates that raged over these bills during the autumn of 1776 in Williamsburg, the young Jefferson revealed his gift for opposing men in principle without personal rancor. Pendleton was, Jefferson said, "one of the most virtuous and benevolent of men, the kindest friend, the most amiable and pleasant of companions."

Jefferson won his fight on primogeniture and entails. However, when he tackled another holdover from the days of royalty, he was rocked back on his heels. This was the "establishment" of the Church of England in Virginia. Under the law, Anglicanism was the official religion of the colony, and every citizen, no matter what his religious belief, had to contribute to the support of the parish church in his vicinity. Theoretically, at least, he was also liable to prosecution for dissenting beliefs.

Jefferson wanted to abolish this system totally and sever all connection between the state and the church. But he soon found himself involved in what he later called "the severest contests in which I have ever been engaged." A bill exempting dissenters from contributing to the established church finally passed. But Pendleton and his allies returned to the fray with a suggestion for a general tax to be distributed to all the churches on a percentage basis. The debate on this and other amendments made it clear that a great many Virginians were determined to maintain some form of religious establishment. The best Jefferson and his supporters could do was fight off the general tax, and the main issue was left for future decision.

In these bruising battles, Jefferson found a new and most welcome ally, a diminutive, scholarly representative from Orange County named James Madison. He was seven years younger than Jefferson, but the two found, almost from the moment they met, that they shared an intuitive union of mind and feeling about politics. Jefferson found himself deeply impressed by Madison's voluminous learning and his ability to apply it successfully to practical matters. Jefferson was also delighted by Madison's ribald wit and fund of droll stories. Above all, he admired Madison's habit of "never wandering from his subject into vain declamation, but pursuing it closely in language pure, classical, and copious, soothing always the feelings of his adversaries by civilities and softness of expression . . ."

While Virginians fought a war of words among themselves, George Washington was fighting a war of bullets with the British in New York. It is hard for the modern reader, accustomed to the idea of total war, in which a nation presses every able-bodied man and woman into service, to understand the eighteenth-century attitude toward war. It was a compartmentalized approach, a belief that those who had the talent and inclination to be soldiers would and should do the fighting while politicians continued to politick and businessmen continued to trade. But grim news from the battlefront made more than one man wonder if this was not a dubious assumption. Harassed by orders from Congress that forced him to fight where defeat was almost a certainty, relying on an army that was half untrained militia who ran at the first shot, Washington was driven out of New York and into New Jersey where his army dwindled to a ragged fragment that fled across the Delaware one jump ahead of the pursuing British.

Letters poured in to the Virginia debaters, abruptly reminding them that the government they were trying to perfect might be stillborn if they failed to support Washington and his desperate men. Jefferson, back at Monticello in mid-December, received a letter from Governor Patrick Henry, appointing him the county collector of blankets and rugs for the freezing soldiers. The message was in itself an ironic comment on the woeful lack of American resources. Like most of his fellow Americans, Jefferson had optimistically pictured the war as a single campaign, perhaps two or three battles fought in the summer and early fall. Washington temporarily rescued the situation from total disaster by slashing across the Delaware on Christmas night 1776 to capture 900 crack German troops at Trenton. A few days later, a brilliant flank march carried him around the overconfident enemy and enabled him to repeat this success against startled British regiments at Princeton. The war settled into a winter stalemate. By now, it was grimly evident to both sides that it was not going to end quickly.

Jefferson spent the winter of 1777 battling the elements and worrying over Martha's health. She was pregnant again. The weather was unbelievably severe for Virginia - the coldest winter in the memory of anyone living. Jefferson's wells went dry, and he was forced to devote hundreds of man-hours to dragging water up the winding road to his mountaintop.

Blocked in the legislature, Jefferson now tried a flank attack on Virginia's religious establishment. He accepted membership on a committee to undertake a general revision of the laws. He himself had proposed the idea, and he willingly shouldered much of the enormous burden. For two years, he toiled on this task, interrupting it only for meetings of the legislature.

In mid-May 1777, Jefferson returned hastily from one of these sessions to be at Martha's side for a now familiar ordeal. For six days, he waited and worried in her bedroom, half-nurse, half-husband. On May 28, his friend Dr. George Gilmer and his sister, Martha Carr, resolutely showed him the door, and he paced the floor of his still unfinished mansion while Martha writhed and gasped in labor. Then the door burst open, and George Gilmer stood beaming at him, holding in his arms a tiny red body swathed in blankets. It was a boy. Thomas Jefferson was at last the father of a son.

The whole plantation rejoiced. Nothing was more precious to a Virginian, with his deep sense of family pride, than a son. Seventeen days later, the words of joy became the ashen taste of sorrow on everyone's lips. Mournfully on the night of June 14, 1777, Jefferson wrote in his little pocket diary: "Our son died 10 H. 20 M. P.M."

Monticello's wells remained dry for the rest of the year, a kind of symbol of the Jeffersons' spiritual desolation. Work on the mansion dragged. Letters drifted in from his friends in Congress. John Adams had written, "We want your industry and abilities here extremely." Adams added a soft rebuke, "Your country is not yet quite secure enough to excuse your retreat to the delights of domestic life."

Not until late August did Jefferson answer this letter that Adams had written to him two days before the birth of the lost son. Richard Henry Lee was more sarcastic, writing, "It will not perhaps be disagreeable to you in your retirement sometimes to hear the events of war and how in other respects we proceed in the arduous business we are engaged in."

To neither of these friends did Jefferson attempt to explain the real reason for his retirement. He could only hint at it in a wistful letter to Benjamin Franklin, written in mid-August. "I wish my domestic situation had rendered it possible for me to have joined you in the very honorable charge confided to you . . ."

In the North, the war thundered on with the same depressing alternation of victory and defeat. Washington lost two desperate battles before Philadelphia, and the British occupied the American capital, sending Congress scurrying westward to York. At Saratoga, another British army led by John Burgoyne blundered into defeat and finally surrendered to the British-born general, Horatio Gates. Jefferson watched hopefully from afar and tried to bury his personal grief in work on the revision of Virginia's laws. His reluctance to leave Martha was evident even in October when he was ten days late taking his seat at the fall meeting of the Virginia Assembly. He may not have planned to come at all, but no less than fifty members had absented themselves and the speaker of the house was forced to order the sergeant at arms to summon the delinquents under threat of arrest for contempt.

For the next eighteen months, while the war stumbled along in the same dreary stalemate, Jefferson gave almost all his time to assembly politics and the immense scholarly effort involved in revising the laws. He played a leading role in whipping through the Virginia legislature a prompt approval of the Articles of Confederation, which created at least a semblance of national unity.

But a continental vision was not enough, in the opinion of the man who was bearing the heaviest burden of the war. In the winter of 1778-79, George Washington wrote to Benjamin Harrison to lament the second-rate men that all the states, including Virginia, were sending to Congress. "Where is Mason, Wythe, Jefferson, Nicholas, Pendleton, Nelson, and another I could name?" (Meaning Harrison himself.) A few months later, Washington pleaded with George Mason, "Let this voice . . . call upon you, Jefferson and others."

For Jefferson, the explanation still lay in the fragile figure who stood in the foreground of his vision of the future at Monticello. On August 1, 1778, he recorded in his notebook, "Our third daughter is born." It had been a repetition of all Martha's previous births, anxiety over her condition before and even more anxiety over both mother and child after the event. Jefferson did not take his seat in the assembly that year until the fall session was almost over. He stayed at Monticello until he was certain that both Martha and the newcomer, whom he named Mary, were out of danger.

In February 1779, Jefferson met George Wythe and Edmund Pendleton, his two fellow law revisers, at Williamsburg. "Day by day," he said, "we examined critically our several parts, sentence by sentence, scrutinizing and amending until we had agreed on the whole. We then returned home, had fair copies made of our several parts which were reported to the General Assembly on June 18th, 1779."

The magnitude of the effort is best summed up by Jefferson's own words: "We had in this work brought so much of the Common Law as it was thought necessary to alter, all the British statutes from Magna Charta to the present day and all the laws of Virginia from the establishment of our legislature . . . to the present time which we thought should be retained, within the compass of 126 bills, making a printed folio of ninety pages only." James Madison later called it "the most severe of his [Jefferson's] public labours." It was, Madison said, "a model of statutory composition, containing not a single superfluous word."

Jefferson's main motive in undertaking this huge job surfaced in his bills on religion and education. Both were bold and sweeping visions of how a free society should organize itself in order to encourage the "natural aristocracy of talent and virtue." To the end of his life, Jefferson believed that his "Bill for Establishing Religious Freedom" was, with the possible exception of the Declaration of Independence, the most important thing he ever wrote. The preamble contains some of his finest, least-known phrases.

> Well aware that the opinions and belief of men depend not on their own will but follow involuntarily the evidence proposed to their minds;

> that Almighty God hath created the mind free and manifested his supreme will that free it shall remain by making it altogether insusceptible of restraint;

> that all attempts to influence it by temporal punishments or burthens, or by civil incapacitations, tend only to beget habits of hypocrisy and meanness, and are a departure from the plan of the holy author of our religion, who being lord both of body and mind chose not to propagate it by coercions on either . . . as was in his Almighty power to do, but to exalt its influence on reason alone;

> that the impious presumption of legislators and rulers, civil as well as ecclesiastical, who being themselves but fallible and uninspired men, have assumed dominion over the faith of others, setting up their own opinions and modes of thinking as the only

true and infallible and as such endeavoring to impose them on others, hath established and maintained false religions over the greatest part of the world through all time;

that to compel a man to furnish contributions of money for the propagation of opinions which he disbelieves and abhors is sinful and tyrannical;

that even forcing him to support this or that teacher of his own religious persuasion is depriving him of the comfortable liberty of giving his contributions to the particular pastor whose morals he would make his pattern, and whose powers he feels most persuasive to righteousness; and is withdrawing from the ministry those temporary rewards, which proceeding from an approbation of their personal conduct are an additional increment to earnest and unremitting labors for the instruction of mankind;

that our civil rights have no dependence on our religious opinions, any more than our opinions in physics or geometry;

that therefore the proscribing any citizen as unworthy of the public confidence by laying upon him an incapacity of being called to offices of trust and emolument, unless he profess or renounce this or that religious opinion, is depriving him injudiciously of those privileges and advantages to which in common with his fellow citizens he has a natural right;

that it tends also to corrupt the principles of that very religion it is meant to encourage by bribing with a monopoly of worldly honors and emoluments, those who will externally profess and conform to it; that though those indeed are criminal who do not withstand such temptation, yet neither are those innocent who lay the bait in their way;

that the opinions of men are not the object of civil government nor under its jurisdiction;

that to suffer the civil magistrate to intrude his powers into the field of opinion and to restrain the profession or propagation of principles on supposition of their ill tendency is a dangerous fallacy, which at once destroys all religious liberty because he being of course judge of that tendency will make his opinions the rule of judgment and approve or condemn the sentiments of others only as they shall square with or differ from his own;

that it is time enough for the rightful purposes of civil government for its officers to interfere when principles break out into overt acts against peace and good order;

and finally, that truth is great and will prevail if left to herself;

that she is the proper and sufficient antagonist to error and has nothing to fear from the conflict unless by human interposition disarmed of her natural weapons, free argument and debate; errors ceasing to be dangerous when it is permitted freely to contradict them.

Then came the statute itself, a prime example of Jefferson's distaste for the superfluous in language, as well as in architecture.

We the General Assembly of Virginia do enact that no man shall be compelled to frequent or support any religious worship, place or ministry whatsoever, nor shall be enforced, restrained, molested, or burthened in his body or goods, or shall otherwise suffer, on account of his religious opinions or belief; but that all men shall be free to profess, and by argument to maintain, their opinions in matters of religion, and that the same shall in no wise diminish, enlarge or affect their civil capacities.

With this declaration of spiritual independence, Jefferson coupled his "Bill for the More General

Diffusion of Knowledge" that aimed at buttressing this freedom with an informed, educated electorate. It not only called on Virginia to set up a public school system but planned it in detail. Jefferson proposed dividing each county into "hundreds" - small neighborhood school districts for the primary level. Above these, the better students would move on to "grammar" schools where a much smaller number of young men of genuine ability would be educated at public expense and, finally, twenty students from these schools would be selected to go on to the College of William and Mary on public scholarships. Those able to afford an education would, Jefferson expected, send their children to these schools at their own expense.

Jefferson regarded these two bills - and the abolition of entail and primogeniture - as the heart of his program for Virginia. "The restoration of the rights of conscience relieved the people from taxation for the support of a religion not theirs; for the establishment was truly of the religion of the rich," he said. The bill for education would enable them to "understand their rights, to maintain them, and to exercise with intelligence their parts in self-government; and all this," Jefferson triumphantly concluded, "would be effected without the violation of a single natural right of any one individual citizen."

Jefferson's vision was too advanced for his contemporaries. The declaration of religious freedom caused such a furor in the assembly practically nothing else was discussed. Nor was it possible to settle the matter for years to come. The education bill was considered too burdensome for Virginia's strapped finances, and not for another eighteen years would even part of it be enacted into law. But Jefferson had created what James Madison called "a mine of legislative wealth" on which he and other Virginians would draw for the next two decades.

5

Young Jefferson

During the first months of 1779, when he was
completing the revisions of the laws, the
war suddenly became much less distant for
Jefferson. Over 4,000 British and German officers
and their troops, captured at Saratoga, were marched
into Albemarle County where Congress thought
there would be more food and less chance of their
escaping. Congress was supposed to have barracks
built and ample food ready for these men when they
arrived. Instead, the prisoners found the barracks
half-finished and most of the food spoiled.

The addition of so many hungry mouths put a
severe strain on the resources of thinly populated
Albemarle, and soon there was talk among
Governor Patrick Henry and his council, no doubt

prompted by more than a few complaining letters, that the troops should be moved elsewhere. The moment Jefferson heard about this idea, he wrote a long letter to Henry, protesting violently "as an American" and "a citizen of Virginia." He especially denounced the plan to separate the officers and men, which would be a direct violation of the surrender terms signed at Saratoga. This, he declared, "would be a breach of public faith." The plan was dropped, and the troops went to work, finished the barracks themselves, and planted gardens. They were soon established in moderate comfort.

For the German and British officers, Jefferson threw open the doors of Monticello, inviting them to dinner, joining them in duets on the violin, and discussing philosophy and science with those who were interested. One young English captain named Bibby later recalled how he and his friends would visit Monticello and almost invariably find themselves pressed into an impromptu musicale, those who could play performing on instruments and others joining in the singing. Bibby said that Jefferson was one of the best amateur violinists he had ever heard. To a studious young German officer named De Unger, Jefferson wrote: "When the course of events shall have removed you to distant scenes of action, where laurels not moistened with the blood of my country may be gathered, I shall urge my sincere prayers for your obtaining every honor and preferment which may gladden the heart of a soldier. On the other hand, should your fondness for philosophy resume its merited ascendancy, is it impossible to hope that this unexplored country may tempt your residence, by holding out materials wherewith to build a fame, founded on the happiness, but not on the calamities of human nature?"

With the two commanding officers, Major General William Philips and Baron de Riedesel, Jefferson was on equally intimate terms, entertaining back and forth at dinner. Riedesel and his wife rented the house of Philip Mazzei, who had returned to Italy. General Philips was so touched by Jefferson's liberal spirit, he wrote him a note of gratitude, to which Jefferson replied: "The great cause which divides our countries is not to be decided by individual animosities . . . to contribute by neighborly intercourse an intention to make others happy is the shortest and surest way of being happy ourselves."

While Jefferson charmed these former enemies, the war seemed to be stumbling along at the same stalemated pace. Most Americans felt time was in their favor. Congress, on February 15, read a report from a committee, proposing peace terms. France had entered the war on the American side, and Spain was making threatening noises toward Great Britain too, all of which seemed to point toward only one conclusion - Britain, convinced that victory was impossible, would give up the struggle.

Only in the south was there some contradictory evidence. A British army had come rampaging up from Florida to capture Savannah and almost totally subdue Georgia. This new strategy lay like a small but ominous cloud on Virginia's horizon when Jefferson received what was, for him, even more alarming news. His friends were nominating him for governor.

6

Jefferson's instinctive reaction to the nomination was refusal. He could barely perform the duties of an assemblyman, meeting for a few brief weeks twice a year. A governor was on duty day-in, day-out for his entire term. But this time his friends were adamant. Edmund Pendleton told him, "You are too young to ask that happy quietus from the public and should at least postpone it till you have taught the rising generation the forms as well as the substantial principles of legislation."

Over Jefferson's protests, Pendleton and others proceeded to put his name in nomination. His chief opponent, ironically, turned out to be his friend John Page, who had served as lieutenant governor under the outgoing executive, Patrick

Henry. Page wanted the job even less than Jefferson. His friends, largely followers of Henry who was already drifting further and further away from Jefferson's ideas, put him forward, and after a rather brisk contest in the assembly (which chose the governor under the new constitution), Jefferson won by a mere six votes. The two friends promptly exchanged cheerful notes assuring each other that there was not an iota of hard feelings on either side.

Six days after Jefferson took office, he was writing to William Fleming, who was serving as a delegate to the Continental Congress in Philadelphia, asking him if there was any truth to the rumor that the British were willing to make peace, but Congress was dragging its feet on negotiation. "It would surely be better to carry on a ten years war sometime hence," Jefferson said, "than to continue the present an unnecessary moment."

Even a cursory look at Virginia's situation made it clear to Jefferson that disaster was imminent. A runaway inflation was on its way to making the paper money issued by the Continental Congress, Virginia, and other states a bitter joke. Jefferson's salary was a princely 375 pounds a month - close to $9,000 in contemporary money. But its purchasing power was another matter. During the first months of his term, he was paying 5 pounds for some pens and 36 pounds for a bonnet for Martha. In

Philadelphia, it took 50 Continental dollars to buy two pairs of shoes.

The galloping inflation was a personal as well as a public disaster for Jefferson. The signers of the bonds he had accepted as payment for the Wayles's debt were able to pay him off in the worthless paper at about two cents on the dollar, and Jefferson found himself faced with paying the debt all over again. The British creditors, who had refused to accept the bonds in the first place, were of course hardly inclined to settle for the depreciated American dollars.

At least as ominous as finances was the condition of Virginia's defenses. Two months before Jefferson became governor, a British fleet had dropped anchor in the Chesapeake and sent ashore 2,000 men who captured with almost ridiculous ease a supposedly reliable seacoast fort, burned the town of Suffolk, and cut a swath of fiery destruction across several dozen square miles of Virginia's Tidewater without losing a man. The ease with which this exploratory raid had been conducted made it almost certain that the British would return.

Simultaneously, Jefferson had to worry about an even more bitter and barbarous war on Virginia's western borders. More than a year before, he and two other assemblymen had been appointed by Governor Patrick Henry to advise a valiant frontier fighter named George Rogers Clark on his plans to combat British-led Indian forays in the Ohio River

Valley. Clark found in Jefferson a companion spirit when it came to a vision of American expansion westward. It was Jefferson more than anyone else who encouraged Clark to assemble the small, compact force honed for frontier warfare that routed the British from the Northwest Territory and created a legitimate American claim to this vast virgin land. But the redcoats were far from beaten. Clark was back in Virginia soon after Jefferson became governor, begging him for more money and munitions. Simultaneously, Congress called on Virginia for more men to fill her Continental battalions and for more money to bolster the sagging Continental treasury. Governor Jefferson was swamped.

Worst of all were the severe limitations on the governor's authority. Elected by the legislature, surrounded by his council, he was little more than the echo of many voices. The framers of the Virginia constitution had been so nervous about potential dictators that they had hedged the executive office with dozens of crippling restrictions. The governor was not expected to initiate policy, only execute what the legislature decreed, and then he had to have the approval of his council for his interpretation. This made for maddeningly slow government when the harsh exigencies of war might demand the utmost speed. Jefferson had no power to stop the state from printing more and more paper money. He could not tighten the lax militia law that enabled men to give almost any excuse and avoid a call to arms. He had no power to requisition horses and supplies if the individuals refused to surrender them.

There was also Martha's health to worry about. Jefferson did not bring her to hot, feverish Williamsburg during the first summer of his governorship. He left her in the cool, familiar shade of The Forest where he visited her at every opportunity. In the fall, Martha and her two daughters moved into the handsome red brick Governor's Palace. There Jefferson no doubt entertained her with reminiscences of his college days when he had been a frequent dinner guest of the cultured royal governor, Francis Fauquier. But the overwhelming amount of work to be done gave the harassed governor little time for his family. He met daily for hours with his council that fortunately included his new friend James Madison, his old friend John Page, and his still older friend from Albemarle, John Walker. There was little they could do but watch the lengthening shadow of war move closer to them. In February 1780, a British fleet and army descended upon Charleston, South Carolina, and trapped a 5,000-man Continental army inside the city. Many of these irreplaceable troops were Virginians, and when the British settled down to a siege, it soon became evident that their capture was only a matter of time.

Charleston fell in May 1780, and the British then moved swiftly to subjugate the rest of South Carolina. On May 29, British cavalry under Lieutenant Colonel Banastre Tarleton, a name that was to haunt Jefferson, wrecked another Virginia regiment at Waxhaws Creek. Virginians shuddered at these blows, which destroyed the cream of their fighting men and swept away tens of thousands of dollars of irreplaceable military equipment. Carping voices began to wonder about the wisdom of letting Virginians fight and die to defend other states when their own shores were all but naked to the enemy. But Governor Jefferson more than proved his vision of the Revolution was continental - no matter how much time he had spent in Virginia.

When Major General Horatio Gates marched south to challenge the British grip on Georgia and South Carolina, Jefferson manfully called out the best of Virginia's militia and committed 800 of these part-time soldiers to bolster Gates's slender 1,200-man force of Continentals. They blundered into the worst disaster of the war. Weakened by bad food and exhausted by an all-night march, the Americans collided with Charles, Lord Cornwallis, near Camden, South Carolina, and were routed by a British bayonet charge. Most of the Virginia and North Carolina militia fled without firing a shot. Gates, on the fastest horse he could find, did not stop retreating until he reached Charlotte, North

Carolina, sixty miles away. The Continentals were wiped out almost to the last man and those militia who were not killed or captured in the pursuit were unlikely ever to volunteer again.

Jefferson could only grit his teeth, apologize for the disgraceful performance of the Virginia militia, and grimly send word to Gates that he was calling on 2,000 more men to join him in North Carolina by September 25. He noted the futility of this brave gesture in the same sentence, with the words, "We have not Arms to put into the hands of these men."

To multiply Jefferson's worries, Martha was pregnant again. The threat of British invasions had inspired the assembly to take a suggestion Jefferson had made in 1776; they finally moved the capital from coastal Williamsburg to Richmond. There Jefferson rented a small wooden house from a relative and set up housekeeping once more with Martha and the two little girls. In the middle of November, Martha gave birth to another daughter, Lucy Elizabeth, and the usual atmosphere of crisis prevailed. But the little girl seemed to thrive, and Governor Jefferson was soon back at his desk, engulfed in the swirling problems of trying to run a war without money.

During these same frantic months, he nevertheless found time to demonstrate his capacity for friendship. James Monroe was a twenty-two-year-old Virginian who had fought with skill and bravery under Washington at Trenton and other battles. Returning to Virginia, he seemed to have experienced one of those crises which many young men of other generations have gone through after fighting a war. He drifted aimlessly, unable to decide on a career until he met Jefferson in 1780. With all that he had to do, Jefferson not only recommended a legal career for Monroe, but worked out a course of study for the young ex-soldier whom he personally supervised.

During the crisis created by the defeat of Gates, Jefferson commissioned Monroe a lieutenant colonel and sent him south to make a personal report on the situation in the southern army. The result of this attention is a seldom-quoted but memorable letter, which is one of the finest tributes to Jefferson ever written.

> . . . A variety of disappointments with respect to the prospects of my private fortune previous to my acquaintance with Your Excellency, upon which I had built as on ground which could not deceive me and which failed in a manner which could not have been expected . . . nearly destroyed me. In this situation had I not formed a connection with you, I should most certainly have retir'd from society with a resolution never to have enter'd on the stage again . . . Believe me. I feel that whatever

I am at present in the opinion of others or whatever I may be in future has greatly arose from your friendship. My plan of life is now fixed, has a certain object for its view and does not depend on either chance or circumstance further than the same events may affect the public at large.

Meanwhile, Jefferson's troubles as governor were just beginning. In early January, he was at work at his desk, when a message, which had unaccountably taken two full days to reach him, arrived from the coast. A British fleet was in the Chesapeake.

Jefferson had no way of knowing that he was about to become the first American to confront Brigadier General Benedict Arnold of the British army. Having failed in his plot to surrender West Point in the fall of 1780, Arnold had escaped to British-held New York where he was given a general's commission and promptly sent south with 1,600 troops. One of the boldest commanders on either side in the entire war, Arnold wasted no time starting up the James River with his army in captured American ships.

Desperately, Governor Jefferson tried to assemble some militia to oppose him, but everything went wrong. In wild haste, Jefferson had to pile his wife and children into a carriage and send them to Tuckahoe. He himself stayed at Richmond until the last possible moment, directing the removal of public records and stores. That night, when everything possible had been done in the deserted capital, Jefferson rode to Tuckahoe and decided the plantation was too close to Richmond for safety. In the early dawn, he took Martha and the three girls across the river and sent them on to another plantation, eight miles farther inland. Martha could hardly have recovered from her pregnancy, and little Lucy was only two months old. Neither was in a condition to become a refugee in the worst of winter.

Though he must have been almost sick with anxiety for Martha and the children, Jefferson turned his horse in the other direction and rode furiously down to Manchester, directly across the river from Richmond. Except for three or four hours' rest snatched at Tuckahoe, he had been in the saddle for most of the previous thirty-six hours, and just before he reached Manchester, his horse collapsed and died on the road. Jefferson had to carry his saddle and bridle on his back until he reached a farmhouse and borrowed an unbroken colt. He rode on to arrive in Manchester in time to see Arnold's red-coated battalions marching down Richmond's main street. Two hundred Virginia militia could only retreat at top speed before the formidable royal force. Jefferson watched in helpless frustration from the other side of the river while Arnold burned the public buildings, tobacco warehouses, and other property. The traitor marched a detachment upriver to Westham, where his men burned the foundry and artificer's shops in which Virginia made its muskets and destroyed most of the public papers that had been left there by some confused waggoneers.

In the midst of his troubles, the public person remained the essential Jefferson. One day, driving hard along a narrow road, he passed a soldier with a huge pack on his back. The footsore infantryman begged Jefferson to give him a lift in his phaeton. Jefferson's mind flashed ahead, warning him that the road was probably full of soldiers, and if he gave them all rides, his already gasping horse might collapse. He said no and drove on, but before he had gone a quarter of a mile, his conscience troubled him so badly that he turned around and rode back in search of the man. But the soldier had turned down a side road, and Jefferson never found him. The memory of this small incident troubled him for years.

On January 7, Benedict Arnold boldly marched his men twenty-five miles back to his ships, waiting for him on the James at Westover, and sailed back down the river, troubled by nothing but a minor skirmish with a detachment led by George Rogers Clark. General Arnold occupied Portsmouth and set up what looked ominously like a permanent base. In March 1781, he was reinforced by 2,000 more men under Major General William Philips, Jefferson's erstwhile Monticello neighbor, who had been exchanged.

Against these 3,000 tough professionals, the distracted Jefferson had nothing but a handful of green Continentals and whatever militia he could induce to risk their lives in such an unlikely contest. At the same time, pleas for aid from west, north, and south continued to bombard the harassed governor. A new American commander in the Carolinas, Nathanael Greene, begged Jefferson for men and material. George Rogers Clark and other westerners warned of impending disaster along the border. Washington needed men if he ever hoped to dislodge the British from their main base in New York.

With all these worries, Jefferson had to endure another wrenching personal loss. At 10:00 a.m. on raw, rainy April 15, five-month-old Lucy Elizabeth died in the rented house in Richmond. Martha was so stricken that Jefferson did not even dare to leave her to walk the few yards from his residence to the brick house where his council met. He sent a note to David Jameson, a member of the council, "The day is so very bad that I hardly expect a council, and there being nothing that I know of pressing, and Mrs. Jefferson in a situation in which I would not wish to leave her, I shall not attend today."

Two weeks later, Jefferson must have shuddered to learn that the British were on the James once more, this time with an army of 2,500 men. Jefferson's only hope was word from Washington that the Marquis de Lafayette was marching south with 1,200 Continentals. The British landed near Williamsburg, routed a body of militia there, and burned a state shipyard on the Chickahominy River. Landing again at City Point where the Appomattox met the James, the British fought a brief battle with 1,000 militia led by Baron Johann von Steuben, drove these amateur soldiers and their commander over the Appomattox, destroyed huge quantities of tobacco and other stores, and burned a number of ships. Another division marched to Chesterfield Courthouse and burned barracks and military stores there. At the same time, Arnold was out on the James, smashing a small flotilla of river boats with which the desperate Virginians attempted to halt his progress up the river. James Monroe, under intense British fire, risked his life to burn several abandoned American ships, rather than have them fall into British hands. This last fight took place at Osborne's, only a few miles below Richmond.

For Jefferson, the defeat had nerve-wracking personal meaning. He had sent Martha and the two remaining daughters fleeing into the country again with orders to await him at Elk Hill. Now the British breakthrough exposed them to capture or worse. There was nothing to stop the enemy from cruising up the James to land at the plantation, whose lush farmlands would immediately catch their marauding eyes. Martha and the girls tried to get across the river (no doubt on Jefferson's advice) and retreat to Tuckahoe but found themselves trapped by an order that had collected all the canoes and boats in the neighborhood to carry grain to the militia army.

His family's plight may have been an added reason why Governor Jefferson resolved to make a stand at Richmond. He was also loath to abandon the considerable amount of tobacco and public stores that had been again collected in the town. His military advisers heartily concurred, and they had concentrated every militiaman they could muster in the little village.

On April 29, these unreliable soldiers were bolstered by the arrival of the Marquis de Lafayette, at the head of a dusty advance column of 900 Continentals. It was the first time the homely, engaging, young Frenchman and Jefferson had met, though they had been corresponding since Lafayette began his march south. It was the best possible way to begin a friendship. The marquis's battle-toughened regulars saved Jefferson from the humiliation of another headlong flight. The next day, the British appeared at Manchester across the river, and after looking at the determined American array on the Richmond bluffs, decided it was the better part of valor to retire down the river and attack more tobacco instead.

But Governor Jefferson's troubles were still far from over. Benedict Arnold sailed back to New York, and Major General Philips died of a bilious fever. They were replaced by the toughest, most aggressive

British general in the war, Charles Cornwallis. He had been fighting Nathanael Greene up and down North Carolina and finally decided that chasing the elusive American was a futile game as long as Greene was able to replenish his battered army with men and supplies from Virginia. The solution to the problem - possibly the solution to the entire war, Cornwallis decided - was an all-out campaign to smash Virginia's spiritual and material resources. He brought with him from the Carolinas enough troops to swell the British army in Virginia to almost 9,000 men - a force that made Lafayette and his puny 1,200 Continentals almost laughable. Lafayette mournfully wrote to Washington on May 24, "I am not strong enough even to get beaten."

The last weeks of Jefferson's governorship were trickling away in an atmosphere of almost total despair and futility. The assembly, having been driven out of Richmond twice, decided to transfer the capital to Charlottesville, which seemed beyond reach of Cornwallis's vengeance. Jefferson sent Martha and the two children back to Monticello and prepared to join them there. The mortified governor could only write one last despairing letter to Washington, begging him for his "personal aid." If Washington came to Virginia, Jefferson was convinced that the militia would rise en masse and drive the British into the Chesapeake.

However, Washington replied that he was

committed for the time being to an assault on New York, which he hoped would force the British to withdraw most of the army in Virginia to reinforce that key bastion. Jefferson's only consolation was the last paragraph of Washington's letter that was testimony from the best possible witness that the weary governor had done his utmost to support the war on a continental scale, even at the risk of weakening Virginia. "Allow me . . . to express the obligations I am under for the readiness and zeal with which you have always forwarded and supported every measure which I have had occasion to recommend through you," Washington wrote.

Long before Jefferson received this letter, the British were on the march again. Lafayette could only retreat before Cornwallis, hoping to wear him down or catch him at a moment when he could strike a damaging, if not a decisive blow. Burning, destroying, and plundering as he went, Cornwallis rumbled through the Virginia countryside while Lafayette and Jefferson watched in helpless dismay.

Virginia's morale dwindled to the vanishing point. Even Jefferson's friend John Page was reduced to despairing gloom. Page told another friend that the British invasions had sunk Virginia "so low in the eyes of the world that no illustrious foreigner can ever visit her or any historian mention her but with contempt and derision . . . I am ashamed and ever shall be to call myself a Virginian."

Jefferson returned to Charlottesville to prepare for the meeting of the assembly while Lafayette wrote desperate pleas to Major General Anthony Wayne, who was mustering reinforcements at York, Pennsylvania. The assembly met on May 24, 1781, and voted Jefferson and his council special war powers that should have been granted to them months before. It was much too late now to rally the prostrate state. For the last three days of Jefferson's term as governor, he and William Fleming, the only member of his council who bothered to attend, met, formally recognized that the governor and his council were in session, and adjourned.

June 2 was the last day of Jefferson's term. But the British were not inclined to let him enjoy his retirement. At dawn on June 4, 1781, a fantastic figure in a scarlet coat, military hat, and plume, came racing up Monticello's winding road on an exhausted horse. Jefferson and several members of the assembly staying at Monticello were routed from their beds to hear wild words tumble from the messenger's lips - Tarleton was coming. The horseman was Jack Jouett, Virginia's Paul Revere. At 11 o'clock on the previous evening, he had been enjoying a drink in a roadside tavern when 180 green-coated British dragoons and seventy red-coated mounted infantry led by Banastre Tarleton himself, Cornwallis's commander of cavalry, thundered up to the doors. Guessing where Tarleton was going, Jouett slipped out a back door, leaped on his horse and while the

British cavalryman allowed his men three hours' rest, Jouett pounded down side roads and over back trails to beat him to Charlottesville.

Jefferson took the news calmly. He summoned a carriage, awakened Martha and the children, and ordered his favorite riding horse taken to Monticello's blacksmith to be shod. The Jeffersons and their guests then had a leisurely breakfast and the assemblymen rode down to Charlottesville to spread the alarm. Everyone mistakenly thought that Tarleton's heavily-armed troopers could not possibly equal Jouett's pace on the road and that they had several hours to spare. They were wrong. Riding all night, Tarleton paused only to burn a few wagons and steal a breakfast from Dr. Thomas Walker, where he also scooped up a member of the Continental Congress. The assembly had barely adjourned, after resolving to meet again at Staunton, farther inland, and many of them were still dallying in town when the green-coated dragoons were upon them. The legislators fled in all directions, but seven of them did not move fast enough, and they, too, became captives.

Meanwhile, underscoring his desire to bag Jefferson, Tarleton had taken the risk of dividing his small force, sending Captain Kenneth McLeod with a detachment thundering up the road from Charlottesville to Monticello. Jefferson, Martha, and the children were still in the house when a patriotic Virginian named Hudson came pounding breathlessly up to the door to tell him that the British were almost to the foot of the mountain. A wild scramble ensued. Martha and their daughters were piled into the carriage, along with several servants and a young Virginian who volunteered to serve as escort, and told to head pell-mell for nearby Blenheim.

It was the third flight in three months for Martha Jefferson, and by far the most frenetic. As she said good-bye to Jefferson, she had no way of knowing if she would ever see him or Monticello again. A hundred possibilities must have swirled through her mind. If the British caught him, they might hang him on the spot or send him in irons to London to be tried for high treason, with the verdict a foregone conclusion. Would they burn Monticello? It was all too possible. What if she herself and the little girls were caught on the road by Tarleton's troopers, infamous for their brutality? No matter how calm her husband was, how soothing his reassurances, this was an hour of terrible anguish for Martha Jefferson.

As soon as his wife and daughters had disappeared down the road, Jefferson rushed back into the house, told two of his servants to hide the silver and any other valuables they had time to grab, and ordered his horse to be brought from the smith's to a point in the road between Monticello and nearby Carter's Mountain. He then left the house on foot and disappeared into the woods, cutting across his own property to Carter's. He picked up his horse and began walking it up the neighboring mountain where he paused and used a telescope he had brought along to study the situation in Charlottesville. He saw no sign of cavalry and decided that Hudson's alarm had been premature. Intending to return to Monticello, Jefferson started back down the mountain to see if he could get some of his private papers out lest the British burn the house. He had gone only a few steps when he noticed that in kneeling down to sight his telescope, he had lost a small dress sword he was carrying at his waist. He went back to search for it and decided, after finding it, to have another look at Charlottesville. In the round eye of the telescope, the main street of Charlottesville was swarming with Tarleton's green dragoons. Jefferson promptly sprang on his horse and cantered into the woods on Carter's Mountain.

The lost sword saved Jefferson's life. Five minutes after he left the house, Captain Donald McLeod and his detachment of dragoons had swarmed up the mountain and were already in possession of Monticello. As the dragoons came up the road, two of Jefferson's slaves, Martin and Caesar, were busy hiding the silver plate and other valuables under the floor of the front portico. At the sound of the British hoof beats, Martin slammed down the planks and trapped Caesar in the dank darkness underneath the porch. Caesar stayed there for eighteen hours without food or water, a testimony to his devotion to Jefferson. Martin was equally loyal. One dragoon shoved a pistol into his chest, cocked it, and ordered him to tell where Jefferson was or he would fire.

"Fire away then," snarled Martin. The dragoon retreated.

For eighteen hours, the British remained in possession of Monticello, but they touched nothing except a few bottles of wine in the cellar. Tarleton had given McLeod strict orders to damage no property, and the command was scrupulously obeyed. The British captain even locked the door of Jefferson's study and gave the key to the slave Martin.

Jefferson, meanwhile, had ridden over Carter's Mountain and joined his family for midday dinner at Blenheim. Later, he sent them to another plantation, nine miles away, and finally took them another seventy miles to Poplar Forest in Bedford County.

Jefferson had escaped British depredation at Monticello, but he was not so lucky elsewhere. While Tarleton drove the governor and the legislators into headlong flight, Cornwallis advanced up the James to the Point of Fork and occupied Jefferson's plantation at Elk Hill. This was richer and more abundant farmland than

Monticello; it was probably the most valuable of all Jefferson's lands. Here, in Jefferson's own words, is what Cornwallis did to the place. "He destroyed all my growing crops of corn and tobacco; he burned all my barns, containing the same articles of the last year; having first taken what corn he wanted; he used, as was to be expected, all my stock of cattle, sheep, and hogs for the sustenance of his army, and carried off all the horses capable of service; of those too young for service he cut the throat; and he burned all the fences on the plantation, so as to leave it an absolute waste." It cost him, he later said, more than the entire 3,700 pounds he owed to his father-in-law's English creditors.

A less scrupulous man might have written off the debt as twice paid, but Jefferson instead wrote the English businessmen a letter, reiterating his intention to pay the money as soon as possible. He was too honest to transfer his own losses to individual Englishmen who had nothing to do with the vicious policy of their government.

At Poplar Forest, meanwhile, Jefferson's misfortunes continued to multiply. One morning, as he cantered out for a ride on his favorite horse Caractacus, the high-spirited animal reared and pitched his master out of the saddle, leaving him crumpled in the dust with a broken left wrist. Jefferson was so badly shaken up that he was housebound for the next six weeks. In this same period of unremitting gloom, he continued to fret over Martha's health. But what seemed like the capstone to his troubles was a report from Staunton where the Virginia Assembly had managed to scrape together little more than a quorum of forty members. A motion had been made and carried recommending an investigation of his governorship.

The motion had been sponsored by one George Nicholas, a young member of the assembly and son of Robert Carter Nicholas, the influential ex-treasurer who had introduced Jefferson's fast-day resolution. The family owned land in Albemarle and had always been friendly to Jefferson. He had no doubt that the man behind young Nicholas was Patrick Henry, who was already beginning to see and think in purely political terms and was not above attempting to destroy, at the first sign of weakness, a rival as potentially powerful as Jefferson. Like a good lawyer, Jefferson demanded a specification of the charges. Nicholas hastily denied that he was making any charges. He was merely asking questions that were on everyone's mind, he claimed, questions that ought to be answered if the people were ever again to have any confidence in their government. Most of the questions that young Nicholas proceeded to scribble off the top of his somewhat empty head concerned the preparation - or lack of it - for Arnold's first raid. The assembly, meanwhile, adjourned until fall, leaving Jefferson dangling between guilt and innocence.

At this point, Congress added another burden to Jefferson's already harassed mind, once more offering him a post in the American diplomatic mission in France. This time the purpose was to participate in the much-rumored, but not yet definite, peace negotiations. The idea must have seemed a little ludicrous to a man who had just felt the hot breath of Tarleton's dragoons. But it was a serious offer, and Jefferson once more had to undergo the pain of refusing his long-cherished opportunity to see Europe, for the same mournful reason. It would have been madness to suggest that Martha Jefferson, after six months as a refugee, could survive a sea voyage in which the chances of capture by blockading British warships would have doubled the dangers of confinement and stale food. Lafayette, through whom the offer passed, did his utmost to persuade Jefferson by dangling promises of introductions to every personage of note in France. Jefferson could only reply that it had given him "more mortification than almost any occurrence in my life" to say no.

7

Partly because of his broken wrist and partly to take his mind off his own misery, Jefferson spent the summer of 1781 writing a book. A member of the French legation in Philadelphia, the Marquis Francois de Barbé-Marbois, had sent him a set of twenty-three questions about the state of Virginia. Jefferson began writing his answers during the six weeks of the summer of 1781 when he was confined to his house by the fall from his horse, and before he stopped he had a 200-page book, which eventually came to be called *Notes on Virginia*. It was an amazing accomplishment for a man who had spent the previous twelve years of his life deeply involved in politics, running a half dozen plantations, building a mansion on a mountain, and worrying over an ailing wife.

Jefferson was candid enough to admit later that he did not simply sit down and dash off so many pages crammed with facts and information relying on what he had in his head. Just as he took careful notes on every aspect of his farming operations, whenever he noticed a particularly interesting fact about any other aspect of life, he was in the habit of jotting it down on a piece of paper. "These memoranda," he said, were "bundled up without order" and difficult to find when he needed one. He decided that Marbois's queries were a perfect opportunity to put them in order and elevate them to the dignity of literature.

The result was a unique book, the most complete and thorough study of America up to that time, and the only one done with an artist's sensitivity, a philosopher's perspective, and a scientist's exactitude. The *Notes* assured Jefferson's reputation as a universal scholar and pioneer American scientist. What other American could discourse in such amazing detail on fauna, flora, geology, natural history, meteorology, Indians, blacks, farming, manufacturing, and government?

Notes on Virginia also glows with Jefferson's love of his country and his deep appreciation of its natural beauty and abundance. Again and again the artist obscures the scientist. The Ohio was for him "the most beautiful river on earth, its current gentle, waters clear and bosom smooth and unbroken."

He became even more lyrical describing the junction of the Potomac and Shenandoah rivers at Harpers Ferry. This was, he said, "one of the most stupendous scenes in nature." Looking down on the "wild and tremendous" clash of waters, breaking through the Blue Ridge on their rush to the sea, the eye through the cleft in the mountain finds "a small patch of smooth blue horizon at an infinite distance in the plain country, inviting you, as it were, from the riot and tumult roaring around to pass through the breach and participate in the calm below." This scene alone, Jefferson declared, was worth "a voyage across the Atlantic."

Intermingled with this proud praise were hundreds of useful facts. The Missouri was "remarkably cold, rapid and muddy. Its overflowings are considerable . . . During the months of June and July a bateau passes from the mouth of the Ohio to the mouth of the Mississippi in three weeks and takes two to three months getting up again. From the mouth of the Ohio to Santa Fe the journey takes forty days."

His most dazzling display of learning was his discussion of Virginia's natural resources. Dividing trees, plants and fruits into medicinal, edible, ornamental, and useful, he listed two dozen in the first category, three dozen in the second, four dozen in the third, and twenty-seven in the fourth. In this section of the book, Jefferson found an opportunity to combine science and spirited pride in his native country. The leading European naturalists, all followers of the Frenchman, Comte Georges de Buffon, who had published a massive series of books on natural history, maintained that "a degenerative" process was at work in North America that made animals and men smaller and punier in size and vitality (and by implication in intelligence as well). Jefferson, the part-time scientist, demolished Buffon by carefully comparing the largest known weights of animals found on both continents. The American elk outweighed his European brother by almost 300 pounds. The American cow was nearly 2,000 pounds heftier, and even the little otter beat out his European relative by 2.3 pounds.

Buffon, determined to prove his degenerative theory, also cast aspersions on the American Indian. The Frenchman's prejudice inspired Jefferson to an eloquent defense of the red man. He was brave; "he will defend himself against a host of enemies, always choosing to be killed rather than surrender." He was "affectionate to his children," and his friendships were "strong and faithful to the uttermost extremity." His "vivacity and activity of mind was fully equal to a white man." To prove this, Jefferson reported the speech of Logan, a Mingo chief, in which the proud old warrior defiantly declared that he had taken up the hatchet because treacherous white men had murdered his entire family. Jefferson, overstating the case a little, declared that no orator in the entire history of

Europe, including Demosthenes and Cicero, could equal Logan's eloquence.

When he reached the subject of "the negro," Jefferson began with a dispassionate, very scientific discussion of his racial characteristics and origins. As a good scientist, limiting himself to his observations, he expressed his doubts about whether the black man was equal in intelligence to the "white man" or the "red man." But he admitted that he had only had an opportunity to study the black man in the degraded condition of the slave.

The mention of this controversial subject brought some of Jefferson's deepest feelings rushing into his prose. He bluntly stated that he favored emancipating all slaves born after a certain date, as he had previously suggested to the Virginia legislature. His picture of slavery was nothing less than devastating. "The whole commerce between master and slave is a perpetual exercise of the most boisterous passions, the most unremitting despotism on the one part and degrading submission on the other . . . The man must be a prodigy who can retain his manners and morals undepraved by such circumstances." For Jefferson, the effect of slavery on whites was as ruinous as its effect on blacks. "With the morals of the people, their industry also is destroyed. For in a warm climate, no man will labor for himself who can make another labor for him." Above all, Jefferson was convinced that slavery threatened the very foundation of American freedom. "Can the liberties of a nation be thought secure when we have removed their only firm basis, a conviction in the minds of the people that these liberties are the gift of God? That they are not to be violated but by His wrath? Indeed, I tremble for my country when I reflect that God is just, that His justice cannot sleep forever."

Those last words had a very contemporary meaning for Jefferson. The summer of 1781 had dwindled to a close, with little apparent change in the military situation in Virginia. Cornwallis had fallen back to the coast, where he began fortifying the small tobacco port of Yorktown, at the end of the peninsula that juts toward the Chesapeake from Williamsburg. Lafayette, with an army still barely one-third the size of the enemy, could do little but maintain a sort of sentinel duty at Williamsburg. It seemed clear that the British were planning to make Yorktown a permanent base from which they could renew their cruel raiding whenever they chose.

In Europe, Russia had offered to mediate the war, and the great powers were making preliminary arrangements for a peace conference, at which England was prepared to claim all the territory in North America over which she could show the British flag with impunity. This would undoubtedly include Georgia, the Carolinas, much of New York, most of Maine, the vast Ohio River Valley, and now, possibly, Virginia.

On August 29, 1781, a man arrived who transformed this doleful scene as dramatically as if he had been an archangel with a fiery sword. A six-foot-two-inch Provencal sailor named Francois Tilly, Comte de Grasse, came booming into the Chesapeake with twenty-nine ships of the line and 3,000 troops from the West Indies. The troops swiftly debarked and joined Lafayette's meager regiments while the warships took up a blockade at the mouth of the York River, their tiers of guns frowning down on the startled British at Yorktown. Meanwhile, around New York, George Washington and another aggressive Frenchman, Comte de Rochambeau, were bombarding the overcautious British commander in chief, Sir Henry Clinton, with a barrage of false intelligence that befuddled him into letting them head south with 6,500 crack troops. Horsemen bearing messages direct from Washington himself pounded through Maryland, calling out every available militiaman, while Jefferson's successor as governor, Thomas Nelson Jr., made equally vigorous efforts in Virginia.

By September 28, an amazing concentration of men and guns had been achieved at Williamsburg. With 20,000 men and more than 100 cannons, Washington rumbled down the peninsula to besiege

Cornwallis behind his incomplete fortifications at Yorktown. After little more than seven days and seven nights of intense bombardment, the fighting earl was forced to surrender the best British army in North America.

Jefferson watched the great event from a distance, learning some of the details from James Monroe. A flash of his feelings about the victory can be glimpsed in his answer to Monroe's remark that Washington ought to have discharged the militia since he had more than enough regulars to do the job. "I think with you," Jefferson wrote, "that the present force of regulars before York might admit of the discharge of the militia with safety. Yet did it depend on me, perhaps I might not discharge them. As an American, as a Virginian, I should covet as large a share of the honor in accomplishing so great an event as a superior proportion of numbers could give." There were, counting sailors, some 28,000 Frenchmen at Yorktown, and only about 10,000 Americans. It was a piece of arithmetic that Thomas Jefferson never forgot.

A few weeks later, Jefferson wrote a revealing letter to George Washington. He would have come in person to congratulate the commander in chief on his victory at Yorktown, he said, "notwithstanding the decrepitude to which I am unfortunately reduced." But he felt that Washington had better things to do than make small talk with "a private individual." This decrepitude could hardly be blamed on a broken wrist that had healed by midsummer. A glance at the original manuscript of this letter suggests another possibility. The draft is crossed out and interlined to an extraordinary degree, suggesting that Jefferson could not concentrate, even to the point of writing a simple letter of congratulation. It is a letter written by a man whose mind was burdened with almost overwhelming anxiety.

Martha Jefferson was pregnant again. After so many years of slow but visible decline in which every pregnancy was a grave crisis, the news must have sent a shiver of foreboding through Jefferson. He also brooded about the so-called charges against his governorship. The charges were so trifling that no man in a better frame of mind would have taken them seriously. In his morbid mood, Jefferson magnified the charges into a fantastic grievance that gave him an excuse to withdraw from public life without confessing either to himself or his friends the real reason. To Edmund Randolph he wrote: "I have returned to my farm, my family, and books, from which I think nothing will ever more separate me."

His friends were utterly astounded by this declaration, and Randolph, serving in Congress in Philadelphia, replied with the first of many remonstrances. "If you can justify this resolution to yourself, I am confident that you cannot to the world."

When the legislature met later in the fall, their attitude made clear the emotional disproportion in Jefferson's view of the charges. When he rose in his seat on December 19 and declared himself ready to meet any and all inquiries, not a word was spoken against him. His accuser, George Nicholas, discreetly absented himself from the chamber. Jefferson then read the list of charges Nicholas had sent him, and his own answers to them, and the House of Delegates unanimously passed a resolution declaring their high opinion of Jefferson's "ability, rectitude, and integrity as chief magistrate of this Commonwealth."

The moment that the assembly voted this exoneration, Jefferson departed for Monticello. Even before he returned, he was again telling friends of his determination never to leave it. "My future plan of life scarcely admits the hope of my having the pleasure of seeing you at your seat," he wrote Horatio Gates, in reply to an invitation to visit that discomfited general at his plantation in Berkeley County. In his desperation, Jefferson almost seemed to believe that his mere presence would be a kind of magic that would give Martha the strength she needed so badly to survive.

He spent the next six months at Monticello, once more half nurse and half companion. Sporadically, he revised his *Notes on Virginia,* expanding the sections on natural history. Early in the spring of 1782, a handsome Frenchman, Major General Marquis de

Chastellux, one of the commanders of the French army at Yorktown, visited Monticello and found Jefferson still working on the book. Although they had corresponded, it was the first time Chastellux and Jefferson had met. The Frenchman's experience was to be repeated by almost everyone who met Jefferson. "I found his first appearance serious, nay even cold," Chastellux said. "But before I had been two hours with him, we were as intimate as if we had passed our whole lives together." Jefferson was not a hail-fellow-well-met, a political backslapper. A man had to prove himself a kindred spirit, worthy of genuine friendship. Once that was decided, there was nothing Jefferson would not do for him. The four days Chastellux spent at Monticello passed, the French aristocrat said, "like so many minutes."

Chastellux gave us one of the few descriptions of Jefferson's house at this point in his life. The ground floor, the Frenchman said, "consists chiefly of a very large lofty saloon [salon] which is to be decorated entirely in the antique style. Above it is a library of the same form. Two small wings with only a ground floor and attic story are joined to this pavilion and communicate with the kitchen, offices, etc., which will form a kind of basement story over which runs a terrace." These words make it clear that Jefferson had not yet entirely completed his mansion, but he had done enough to impress Chastellux. "Mr. Jefferson is the first American who has consulted the fine arts to know how he should shelter himself from the weather," Chastellux wrote. Summing up his host, Chastellux called Jefferson "an American who without ever having quitted his home country is at once a musician, skilled in drawing, a geometrician, an astronomer, a natural philosopher, legislator and statesman . . . It seemed as if from his youth he had placed his mind, as he had done his house, on an elevated situation from which he might contemplate the universe."

Chastellux barely mentioned Martha Jefferson, and it is evident that he saw little of her. By now, she was far advanced in her pregnancy, and one evening he noted that she retired early, leaving Jefferson and his guest to discover a mutual enthusiasm for Ossian. With a bowl of punch at their side, they proceeded to read favorite passages from the rude bard of the north to each other until "the night far advanced imperceptibly upon us." Surely this was an experience that Martha Jefferson, with her love of literature, would not have missed if she had been in good health. When Chastellux departed, Jefferson persuaded him to ride eighty miles farther into Virginia to see the Natural Bridge. However, he accompanied the Frenchman only to the ford of the Mechum River, sixteen miles away, because, as Chastellux put it, "his wife [was] expected every moment to lie in."

A few days after the Frenchman departed, Martha

Jefferson gave birth to a very large baby girl; tradition places the weight at sixteen pounds. Undoubtedly at her request (and it is a sign of how deeply she grieved over her losses), the baby was named Lucy Elizabeth, after the little girl who had died during the months around Richmond.

Now began the four most terrible months of Jefferson's life. Martha simply did not rally after this last exhausting birth. Day by day, she became weaker and more wasted, her steady decline in anguishing contrast to the blooming spring and summer outside her bedroom windows.

Two days before the birth, Jefferson abruptly declined his seat in the House of Delegates, to which the citizens of Albemarle County had elected him. James Monroe, who had been elected a delegate from another county, wrote him as a friend, to let him know that the assembly was strongly critical of his decision. Again, no one knew the real reason because, once more, Jefferson could not bear to state it, even to himself.

The Speaker of the House of Delegates, John Tyler, added a more impersonal and sharper note warning Jefferson that the house "may insist upon you to give attendance" and added a warning about the "censure of being seized." It was within the power of the House of Delegates to send a sergeant at arms to Monticello and drag Jefferson to Richmond under arrest.

By now, Jefferson was in such a state of anxiety, he was almost incoherent. He wrote Monroe a long passionate letter, arguing his right to refuse the position and referring in bitter terms once more to the temporary censure that the House of Delegates had cast on his governorship. The experience had inflicted on him injuries, he vowed, which would only be cured "by the all-healing grave." At the end of this wild diatribe Jefferson remarked, almost as if it was an afterthought, "Mrs. Jefferson has added another daughter to our family. She has been ever since and still continues very dangerously ill."

Monroe, in his reply, proved himself a discerning friend. He ignored Jefferson's disquisition on his right to refuse public service and replied with a touching letter, telling Jefferson he was "much distressed" to hear of Martha's illness. He referred to her affectionately as "our amiable friend." (Martha had been very kind to the lonely young ex-soldier on his visits to Monticello.) Monroe assured Jefferson "that nothing will give me so much pleasure" as to hear of Martha's recovery. Only in a postscript did he tell Jefferson news that was very important to Monroe personally - he had been elected to the governor's council, quite an honor for so young a "parliamentary man." He hoped that Jefferson, "as soon as circumstances will permit you," would let him seek his advice "upon every subject of consequence."

Jefferson did not even answer this letter written at the end of June 1782. He spent the rest of the summer in a torment of soul, watching Martha slowly waste away. His sister Martha Carr and Martha's sister, Elizabeth Eppes, were in the house, but Jefferson did most of the nursing himself. For hours, he sat by Martha's bedside reading to her from their favorite books, and when she slept he retreated to a small room, just outside the bedroom, where he drove himself to forgetfulness by working on his revisions of the *Notes on Virginia*. Years later, his daughter Martha, who had been ten at the time, recalled that Jefferson was "never out of calling" during the four mournful months that her mother lingered.

These two deeply intelligent, sensitive human beings could not conceal from each other, no matter how hard they tried, that each knew what was happening. One day toward the end, Martha could not bear the truth unspoken any longer. She took a pen from her bedside, and wrote on a piece of paper words from their favorite book, *Tristram Shandy*, which the author, Laurence Sterne, himself a dying man, had written to someone he loved.

Time wastes too fast: every letter

I trace tells me with what rapidity

Life follows my pen. The days and hours

Of it are flying over our heads

Like clouds of windy day, never to return -

More everything presses on -

This was as far as her strength could take her. Her faltering handwriting ends with these words. But she knew the rest of the passage as well as Jefferson. Perhaps only a few hours later he took the paper and completed it in his stronger, bolder hand.

- and every

Time I kiss thy hand to bid adieu,

Every absence which follows it, are preludes to that eternal separation

Which we are shortly to make!

On September 6, 1782, Martha Jefferson slowly slipped away from her husband's desperate grasp. In the last anguished hours, she made an emotional request, a compound of love and old fear. She asked Jefferson to promise her that he would never marry again. More than death, she dreaded the thought of her three little girls being raised by a stepmother. To Martha, that word was synonymous with unhappiness. Her own father had married soon after her mother's death, and her girlhood had apparently been troubled by the hostility of a woman who had no love to give a child of a previous wife.

Jefferson, of course, agreed, but he begged her

not to say such things. She was not dying. She could not be. Even now, he was unable to face the terrible truth. As Martha sank into a coma and her breath became the shallow, labored gasps of the dying, Jefferson blacked out. He would have toppled to the floor beside her bed if his alert sister, Mrs. Carr, had not caught him. With the help of Martha's sister, Elizabeth Eppes, Jefferson was half carried, half dragged into the library, where he lost consciousness completely.

For a while, the agitated women thought he, too, was dying. It took the better part of an hour to revive him, and then his grief was so terrifying that fear of death was replaced by fear of emotional collapse. For three weeks, he did not come out of the library. Up and down, up and down, he paced hour after hour, collapsing only, as his daughter put it in her recollection, "when nature was completely exhausted." Occasionally, little Martha would tiptoe into the room, obviously sent by her aunts in the hope that she would remind Jefferson that life had to go on and that he still had responsibilities. But the sight of the little girl at first only brought on even wilder paroxysms of grief. Writing fifty years later, Martha Jefferson said, "The violence of his emotion . . . to this day I do not trust myself to describe."

Jefferson's sensitivity and his devotion to Martha explain, in part, this almost incredible grief. But it seems necessary to add other factors that had run like a dark thread through the years of his married life: guilt over the time he gave to pursuing a reputation as a public and political man and fear, even dread, that the long separations and frantic flights from British raiders to which he had exposed her were the real reasons for Martha's death. He had sacrificed her to the Revolution, and for what? All he had gotten in return was a blotted name for his supposed failures as a war governor. It was this tangle of grief and guilt that drove Jefferson to the brink of insanity.

After three weeks, he finally emerged from the library - still a haunted, driven man. All he could do was ride hour by hour around the countryside, always taking the least-frequented roads, and as often leaving these to blunder through the woods. It was in these weeks that ten-year-old Martha Jefferson became a woman. She reached out to this reeling, incoherent man, this stranger, and offered herself as a wordless companion on these rambling, aimless rides. It was the beginning of a bond between father and daughter that was stronger and more meaningful to both than a marriage.

On October 3, Jefferson wrote a letter to Elizabeth Eppes, who had returned to her home. He told of Patsy (Martha) riding with him five and six miles a day and asking his permission to accompany him on horseback when he went to visit Elk Hill. "When that may be, however, I cannot tell, finding myself absolutely unable to attend to anything like business," Jefferson said. Then his grief burst uncontrollably onto the page: "This miserable kind of existence is really too burthensome to be borne and were it not for the infidelity of deserting the sacred charge left me, I could not wish its continuance a moment. For what could it be wished?" He did not write another letter for almost eight weeks.

Martha Jefferson was buried beneath the great oak on the side of the mountain near Jefferson's friend Dabney Carr and the bodies of her lost children. Over her grave, on a plain horizontal slab of white marble, Jefferson placed the following inscription:

To the memory of Martha Jefferson,

Daughter of John Wayles;

Born October 19th, 1748, O. S.

Intermarried with

Thomas Jefferson

January 1st, 1772;

Torn from him by death

September 6th, 1782;

This monument of his love is inscribed.

Beneath these words, he placed a quotation, in Greek, from the *Iliad*.

If in the house of Hades men forget their
dead

Yet will I even there remember you, dear
companion.

The most deeply felt dream of Jefferson's life was
over. The figure who stood "always in the forefront"
of his vision of happiness was dead. It is easy to
understand why he embraced this vision. It is
harder, but necessary, to pronounce it an essentially
selfish dream. It would have resolved the warfare
that flickered in Jefferson's personality between the
scholar and the man of action, the theorist and the
realist, in favor of the pale life of the mind.

Jefferson, like all men, needed a personal vision to
give order and direction to his life. It had to be a
vision that satisfied his equally demanding head
and heart. Could he find one that would replace
what he had lost? Wandering the Albemarle hills,
pacing Monticello's cheerless rooms, he simply did
not know.

It would take almost a decade for him to realize that
the words he had written in Philadelphia about the
pursuit of happiness by free men required constant
defense and interpretation if they were to become the
guiding spirit of a new nation. Even then, he would
only begin to realize that these words must be lived,
spelled out act by act in the harsh harassing world of
politics if they were to have meaning to men.

Gradually, as Jefferson learned these things, these words would become a new, more generous vision that would ultimately fill - and fulfill - his life.

Made in the USA
San Bernardino, CA
08 May 2018